Awaken the Secret Within

D0770112

Awaken the Secret Within

Keys to Joyful Living

Anne E. Angelheart

iUniverse, Inc.
New York Bloomington Shanghai

Awaken the Secret Within
Keys to Joyful Living

iUniverse books may be ordered through booksellers or by contacting:

iUniverse
1663 Liberty Drive
Bloomington, IN 47403
www.iuniverse.com
1-800-Authors (1-800-288-4677)

Because of the dynamic nature of the Internet, any Web addresses or links contained in this book may have changed since publication and may no longer be valid.

ISBN: 978-0-595-49511-5 (pbk)
ISBN: 978-0-595-61132-4 (ebk)

Printed in the United States of America

Contents

Preface

My journey so far on this Earth has been rich with knowledge and I have had great teachers in my life that have assisted me to be much wiser. I came into this world with a heightened intuition and a talent for seeing truth and to be able to see inside the hearts of others. This led me on a journey to seek out the truth. I was curious about all peoples.

To do this, I studied many religious belief systems since I was fifteen years old. These studies ranged from many types of Christian religions to Buddhism, Taoism, Shamanic in both Native American cultures and Hawaiian, just to mention a few. I have attended many workshops on inner child healing, self-exploration, and psychic phenomena. I studied and became certified in many healing modalities, which I now teach.

By my early thirties, I started sharing what I had learned with others by teaching classes. I creatively combined what I have learned from my teachers and my experiences on my own journey. I began to use my ability to see into the hearts of others and my intuition to help guide people on their paths and remove blocks in their lives allowing them to move forward. Through my experiences teaching workshops and giving spiritual guidance, I was asked for many years to coach one on one with people. So many people started asking for my help that I became a transformational coach in my mid-forties.

Taking all I have learned from the eighteen years of teaching and guiding others, I have learned even more about the tools that we can use in life and how the laws of the universe work on a deeper level. I have continued to share this information through teaching workshops in many areas of life. Goddess weekend is one of my more popular workshops for empowerment. I have mentored many one on one using the techniques in this book. I also had a PBS show for two years and wrote for 2 years for a New Age magazine.

My greatest teacher in this lifetime has been the Mother Earth and all my experiences on this journey of walking on my path.

Acknowledgements

There are so many people I would like to thank that have assisted me in one way or another to birth this book. There are too many to list here that dedicated time, energy, gifts, finances, support and other means to make sure this dream came true. You know who you are and I am very grateful and with an open heart thank you all.

I would like to thank my daughter; Naomi Christianson who has been an inspiration to this book, has shared many insightful ideas, and has dedicated countless hours, days, weeks, and months into making sure this book not only was complete, but that it stayed in its true form and reflected my teachings and heart. I want to thank my daughter, Gillian Ceja for researching, adding ideas, and also dedicating countless hours in making sure this book was a success. I thank my son, Mathew Gutierrez for assisting me in the last half of the book and providing all the graphics. I want to thank Susan Barnes for motivating me to write this book and other assistance in making sure I stayed focused on it. Also, thank you Maureen for endless hours of editing and research work that went into this project.

I thank my dear friend Sandi for all of her support emotional, funding the book and the venting she endured of the frustrations and details of the process of putting this together. I thank Ro and Reecy for all their help in making sure the rest of my life and work ran smoothly while trying to get this baby born.

Many thanks to all of my clients and students who requested this book and provided years of encouragement to produce the book. I want to thank all my teachers, friends and loved ones for providing my lessons in life that led to the wisdom of this book today.

I cannot express in words all my gratitude and the love I have felt from everyone. I feel blessed to have all of these wonderful souls in my life and to have all of their energy in this project.

My deepest thanks,

Anne Angelheart

My Passion

I wrote this book to share my teachings with a larger audience. It is my passion to assist others and to see them grow and become unlimited in life. My passion is to see someone realize what a wonderful bright soul they are and to recognize their worth here on the planet. This book will provide tools that will assist each unique individual to walk awakened on their journey in life. I intend that this book will open the true hearts of all who choose it in their life and will be a great companion to walk with them on their path through life.

This book is full of keys to open the doors to the secrets within. The secrets within that enable you to create a joyous life, and unlock the doors that lead to your authentic self. I wish to show people it is really <u>NO</u> secret at all, that all of this information has always lived within them. The authentic self already knows your fullest potential. The secrets within that awaken will allow you to discover unlimited-ness in all areas of your life. Blessings on your walk through this experience called life.

Anne Angelheart

A Sharing of a Time in my Personal Journey

I wanted to put this in my book because so many people that I have shared it with over the years have told me it put words to what they felt like on their journey at times. It does not mean everyone will experience this but it was one of my experiences when working on going deep into my layers.

In 1984, I had started a journey into myself, reaching deep into my fears, my illusions, and my heart to get to my true nature. I had already done a lot of inner work on myself and yet I felt I had not reached the core of my True self. I was working with a Kahuna (Hawaiian Shaman) at the time and he would give me meditations or exercises to do for going deeper within myself. These exercises or meditations would be to assist me in getting in touch with all my aspects within, release and shed the false parts and come to know the real me inside. For example one the exercises was where he took me to a field, which had fruit trees. With a look of contemplation, he ran an open palm under each piece of fruit. After doing this with several pieces of fruit on the tree, he stopped at one and held his palm about five inches under the piece of fruit. Then as I watched, the fruit just dropped in his hand. He asked me, "Anne, why do you think this has happened?" I thought on this for days and returned to tell him excitedly, "You used Chi and asked it to give itself to you." Well, that was not the answer. Finally, after many days and several different answers that I had given him, and each time he said go deeper, he finally told me what it was. He said, "Anne what is the fruits purpose? To become ripe and when it does it returns to the Mother Earth by dropping from its limb. It then goes into the mother replenishing her and leaving seeds for new growth. I only asked which one was ready to fulfill its purpose."

There were many times such as these that I would come back to him so proud thinking I had found the answer only to hear him say, Go Deeper Anne. One of the times he said, "Go Deeper," I judged myself and wondered if I had done any work at all. I felt frustrated; I took this comment as not getting the answers to my life, when I had felt I did already go deeper. I went home and just wanted to cry. Yet, in the way I was feeling at the time I was throwing what I call one of my human tantrums, babbling aloud how I did get it, the answer, and what does he mean deeper? There were a few more choice words in there also. Once I was done with my human tantrum, I calmed down and decided to meditate on going deeper and what the heck that means. This is what I experienced in that journey and of course the pond is the inner me. The story here is about going through the different layers of self, moving through the illusions, and still traveling deeper to the core, the true inner self. The only thing that makes our true self seem a secret is that we keep our core self a secret to our own self. I hope it helps whoever resonates with this story.

"The Pond"

I sat looking at the surface of the pond, thinking to myself how shiny and beautiful it was. I threw a pebble into the center and watched the ripples move out to the edge and then gently return to the center. As I did this, I could hear my teacher's words in my head, "It's like these ripples on the pond, Anne. Whatever it is you send out into the world, eventually returns again to us."

I threw another pebble, only this time a much larger one. I wondered where that pebble had gone to because I could not see it any longer. Again, I heard my teacher's words in my head, "Go Deeper." How I learned to hate these words, mostly because I did not understand where this "Deeper" was.

Now looking at this pond, I realized DEEPER was like the rock, it is where I could no longer see. I was paying attention to how I was looking at the surface and how the clarity and the shine of it was actually an illusion. I realized the surface was how my perception was at that moment. But where does the foundation come from that enables me to create from what I do now? So, I jumped into the pond, working myself down, down deeper to the bottom to find what was below the surface, below the illusion.

I began the journey and following my natural pattern, just dove in headfirst. There was no wading in, no testing the water with my foot, just plain dove in headfirst. Moving down through the pond of life, I found that this pond of inner self was full of memories. I moved backward in time through the herstory of my life. I felt I was watching old films, ones I could relate to from my experiences, but the person I was viewing (me) seemed to be someone else. I watched these pictures at times unattached, other times I felt I was reliving the experience. These memories were filled with love and joy at times, at other times pain and sorrow, but learning was in all of them. When I felt it was too painful I would return to the surface to breathe and to recuperate. Oh yes, I also all too comfortably step back into the illusion. Then the call of curiosity would vibrate my surface and again I would go back down, back inside, searching for the bottom. It seemed pretty murky and difficult to see the bottom, so I just kept searching downward for the bottom.

I really do not know the Self, so I feel I am venturing into the unknown, and still do not understand where this "deeper" ever ends. As I move through this pond of life, I feel the waters of my life vibrate and move all around me. The vibrations that are occurring down here in the deep are also causing reactions I can see at the surface. The water moves away from my body as I push down further yet it returns quickly to hug at my body again. The deeper I go, these vibrations seem to feel much stronger, and they return feeling stronger, more intense as if a lot of pressure within me. The memories and the emotions attached to them feel so much more intense here. Do I really want to go here? Am I sure, I really want to do this, and if so, why? I break water as I desperately reach back for the surface, for the safety, for the illusions. I push my way back to this place of safety; I gasp for air and feel the relief of being back in a familiar and comfortable place. When I looked around in this comfortable space, it no longer was the same. It all had changed. Was I really gone that very long? In my head, I heard again, "From where? This place has not changed, you have. You looked into and journeyed through the murky waters, your eyes and heart straining to see through to the bottom, and now on your return, you see this place through new eyes and a new heart. The illusion you had is fading. Now go down child, and go deeper." I heard a loud scream in the distance to find that it was only an echo of me. He, my teacher, has to be kidding! I almost did not make it back this time and he wants me to go back, go deeper? My lungs were bursting, my heart pounded with pain, my mind was flooded with thoughts, my body weighted with fears, and I literally had to fight to get back here, back to the familiar. No Way! I am not going back; I am not going in any deeper.

As I began to walk around this new familiar place but as a new me, the call to go back down was getting loud. The pull to go deeper was becoming irresistible. It felt as if someone had a great grip on my feet and was pulling me downward. I fought this until I could not fight anymore. The pull being too strong I surrender to it, and somewhat still reluctant I go deeper. I go ever so deep, this time it is easier to reach the bottom. When I finally arrived at the bottom, I felt as if I was drowning in the place of emotion. My chest felt crushed, my head swimming with thoughts, and I am so very afraid. I fight these feelings and I struggled to return to the surface. Growing very tired, I cannot fight it anymore and I cannot seem to return to the surface. In my frustration and weariness, I began to cry. As I lay there crying, letting go of all of this pain and fear that I know I have carried buried deeply for some time, I start to feel a relief. Then after a moment or so, I feel a great relief and a calm come over me. I felt peace in my heart, I do not remember when I felt this last. I then heard my own voice, "It's ok, the fight is over, and you don't have to struggle anymore. It is that easy, just let it go, it is alright."

The waters felt as if they had swirled around my body as if to hug and caress me. I floated in that tranquility, thankful for the peace, thankful for the release. I look over and there I find the rock, thank God, I am actually here at the bottom! Then I hear, "Go Deeper." At this point, I am feeling too calm and tired to fight or scream. I blow out the last bit of air I still carried with me from the surface and when I do I release the last bit of illusion I carried here with me, the last bit of safety. At that moment, I know it was also an illusion that my world I carried was safety. There was no safety in the illusion. It is funny, but I feel lighter, I hear better, I can see clearly through the water now! I reach out to pick up the rock, and it moves. I reach again and the rock moves again only this time the bottom of the pond begins to move and before I know it the bottom is stirring and my rock is being covered by dirt and sand. Again, I hear those words, "Go Deeper," and I know I am hearing my teacher. I am hearing myself. I no longer need the surface or the illusions that the surface offers. I now feel a little bit of fear rise in me, but I know I cannot go back; I can only go in and go on. I follow the rock and as I do, I find the rock has gone through the earth of the pond of life. I move through this earth and I feel its warmth and its nurturing life, and as I emerge through the bottom, I am surprised to find another world. I find deeper! I find a brilliant light of gold and I find where I end and where I began, I find the true Self, the self that does not belong to the surface, which is not owned by any illusions, or to any physical teacher or teachings. It belongs to no one and no thing, It just Is! It is "I"

I see all, I see nothing, I know all, and I know nothing.

Then I am called to return to the world of the surface. Now, it is that I do not want to leave this place. However, I return knowing this is where I need to be for now. With the illusions removed, I move and breathe in this world without ever really moving. I do without doing. I create without creating. I know all directions are going back as all directions are also going forward. I know there really are no differences, and I know because I Just Am.

Keys to Open the Door

Instructions on how to use this book to successfully create Joy in your life!

I have designed this book to assist you in working with all aspects of yourself and to balance Mind, Body, and Spirit. You will find wisdom within these pages of shared stories, breaking down concepts, and how to mentally review your life. Then in working with the emotional side, you will also explore your inner child. There are tools in here for spiritual reflection and active tools to make your life the joyous one you deserve. Many of these exercises are provided at the end of the chapters with graphics that are designed to help bring out the inner child in you. They are simple and creatively made child like, and I ask that you allow the child to come out when you work with these and be inspired to buy a tablet and draw some of your own. These are just a few to get you started. Think of it as a "fun book" rather than a "work book."

To effectively use the tools within these pages you must stretch out of your box and linear thinking. Play with graphic fun tools and set time aside to work with the more meditative and the self-exploration tools. All of them are designed so that at any time in your life, you feel stuck or at a pause point, you can go back and find the right tool to work with the situation at that time. At the beginning of each chapter are listed the keys to open the door to each specific place in your life you are working on, so it will be easy to go and find the tools at a later time, just checkout the keys and you are there.

So curl up in a blanket, run a hot bubble bath or get your crayons out and enjoy the journey, the most joyful path way!

Part I

Past

Our past makes us who we are today but many aspects of our past need to be healed and released so we can move into a healthier life. We are going to explore ways to become conscious of any parts of our past that keep us stuck in our present life. On this journey, we will also rediscover areas of our past that are positive and help us recognize our strengths and our talents. Many of which we may have forgotten about.

So let us put our seat belts on and travel through memory lane.

Keys to Awaken to the Journey

- How Do You Live Your Life?
- How to Actively Make Choices on a Daily Basis
- Release Learned Programs and Labels in Layers
- Simple Tools that Aid in Transformation
- Discover Who You Really Are
- Remember Who You Were

Awaken to the Journey

When I speak of the journey, I mean your walk here on the earth that is your life and how you live it. I know if you have been drawn to read this book, whether you bought it or it was a gift, the very fact that you are reading these pages says that on some level you have already awakened or are looking to awaken and are looking for the tools to move forward. Your soul has brought you and this information together. To be awake in life is to feel and live life fully and to understand that you choose your reality and are aware of all that is occurring in your life. Experiencing your walk here is being awake.

In the following pages are tools that are keys that will lead you to doors that unlock the secrets within you. You are going to go on an inner journey and each chapter will lead you to another door and another level inside of you. Each level will give you a new perception of yourself, your life, and the world around you. It is a journey of self-discovery. The destination is to BE your true authentic self. You will learn what that means on this journey.

On this journey, you will discover programs that you have acquired in your experiences so far in life. You will examine which ones are healthy for you to have and which are programs you would like to release. You will look at what needs to be released and healed inside of your mental and emotional self, so that you can remember how to be in touch with your soul self. As you become more in touch with your authentic self, you will discover what you really want in life and the tools to help you get there.

When you become clearer about your self, you can then look at what you want to manifest in your outer world and take actions that will get you there. There will be tools to assist you in manifesting your dreams and how to be unlimited in this world. As you read these pages, remember each journey is unique, some tools will work for you, and some will not. We are all different and we all walk our journeys at our own pace, so no judgments on the self. Just take what resonates with you from this journey and let go of what does not. Some things you read in here may not speak to your inner being at this time, but there will be a message for you somewhere in these pages or you would not be reading it. Then in a month or two, or more, you may pick up this book and a completely different part will speak to you and your life at that time and different tools may be the ones you need that time around. So explore You and feel what works and what does not and just have fun with this, as our journeys should have Joy in them.

Many of the tools may seem too simple while others challenging. I hope to break many of the myths out there on HOW one should or should not be when they are considered spiritual or on their spiritual path. Spirituality is NOT religious; it is being in touch with ones own soul and walking your path according to your lessons here on Earth. There are no right or wrong ways to walk your path, just more joyful or less joyful. We all have choices on our journey and we all are accountable for our choices in this life so only you can know what is spiritual to you.

Many times, you hear things like smoking, having a drink, eating foods that are not all organic are things that are not spiritual and that your energy is not clear if you participate in any of the above. Yet, in the same breath, many that are saying this are missing that they are being judgmental and ego based to think that they know the only one true spiritual way. If your soul is here to learn about your body, or you have food issues, who is to say you are not doing what you need to for your own self to learn your lessons? On the journey of self-discovery be gentle with yourself and know your learning and choosing the tools that work best for you. These tools may change as you grow, so be patient, and know that it is all right.

Therefore, you may wonder where the journey ends. For me ~ Never. It is a continuous journey through all experiences and having them in many different ways so as to learn even more from them. I believe we are all seeking our true self, what I call the true heart—the authentic self.

I am referring to our soul self, the part that knows and remembers all the universal laws and how to apply them. The self that knows we are all accountable for our choices and that we all create our own life and experiences. Our birthright is to be whole, healthy, happy, and abundant in all areas of life.

So, how did we forget?

There are many different theories and beliefs on this and I do not want to go over them all since it is a personal journey to your own core beliefs. You will find that answer within yourself as you work on using the keys to unlocking the doors to your inner secrets, secrets we keep from ourselves. I do know, it is layers of programs we have attained over our existence and experiences here on earth that have shadowed the true authentic self from our self.

Layers of the self are invisible shields within us that we have created whenever we had a life changing experience and we created a rule/belief for our self or the world around us. Walking in your true heart is to shed the entire negative programs that we have learned through out life but to realize although we recognize them as negative we still have learned from them. Taking all the layers of the person you are today based on those rules and shedding them, and seeing those experiences as the gems they were as our teachers. Finding out how you really think and feel based on going deep inside yourself and experiencing your true self for the first time, without being tainted by what you were taught growing up.

When you were growing up, you made choices, sometimes called rules within you, based on your experiences in life. One of my rules was about guarding my heart. After living in an environment that did not support sharing your feelings and with individuals who never told the truth, I made the rule that I could not be open with my feelings because it was too vulnerable. In my growing up years, I learned not to trust. In that rule, the outcome was to tell myself "I will never feel that again, or I will never let someone make me feel vulnerable again." Therefore, I made myself stuff my feelings and I never believed what people around me told me. Instead of believing all people were truthful until they prove themselves wrong, my rule was everyone lies until I am convinced they are truthful. These created layers result in a not true self but a created self, based on those experiences and rules. They were rules that served me at the moment and made me believe I was protected. However, a layer is a layer, so when I put my heart shield up to keep hurt out, I also kept deep love out as well.

We make rules for self-preservation. We do not realize how much they have a domino effect and keep us from other experiences in our lives. So as we do this, we in a way begin the process of falling asleep or numbing out. We fall asleep by forgetting that our right is to be healthy, happy, and loved. We numb by stuffing feelings and protecting ourselves so we are not fully feeling and living our life to its fullest. To wake up is to re-look at those rules, understand why we made them, heal them, and make new choices. More people than ever are being touched within and inspired to seek out their true authentic self.

This awakening is really a re-awakening, it is moving from walking unconscious in life to living consciously. It is learning that we always knew the secret because it is within us and always has been. Awakening the secret is exactly that—***awakening*** to what we forgot or became unconscious of in life. Once we realize our true core self we will also realize we always knew all the universal laws including the Law of Attraction. We just became unconscious of it.

One of the reasons so many are doing this right now is that the planet itself is evolving. People are opening more and more to a new and wider vision. The world is changing its perceptions and because of this, the world is ready to hear a different way to take the journey. People are ready for different ways to open their heart and to heal.

Walk Your True Heart

There are many ways to open and awaken the true heart and many tools of the past have been beneficial in doing that. The many tools that have worked were tools we could be open to accepting because of where we were as a consciousness. The world as a whole grows and changes perception as we do as individuals and because of this, energy on the planet is very different now. People are more open to self-awareness and the inner healing process. Television shows are changing and ones that have been around for a long time are moving to a new level. Have you watched Oprah lately? I have known and could tell by how her shows were changing that she was awakening and being self-aware, this started around 1987. I remember my daughter and her girlfriend rushing home from school to watch the show. I could see the change and knew she was going to make great changes in the future for many. She has built a reputation of respect so when she shares a message people are more open to look at what she presents. She had the makers of the Secret (Law of Attraction DVD) on her show, and in doing so that was saying that people were ready to hear it, ready to realize the next level.

It is an exciting time on the planet right now.

In all my experiences of attending workshops on inner work, and now teaching them for many years, I have noticed people just awakening are moving through their inner healing process much quicker than in the past. As the consciousness of the people on this planet was growing and changing, so was the planet itself. It may seem hard to think that energy on the planet can change and be more rapid. Actually, it is a higher frequency, a higher vibration, and a higher tone, which means accelerated. We will talk later about energy on this journey. It isn't so hard to imagine this if you think about how more and more you hear people say, "My Gosh, where did this year go?" or "I don't seem to have enough time in a day, they fly by." It is because the planet Earth is vibrating at a higher rate, which in turn causes things to be accelerated. The great news is we can wake up and heal at an accelerated rate.

Another way to look at this is to think of a journey and how people had to travel from one place to another by foot and how it took them a long time to get there. Then when they saw a horse as a tool for transportation, they could make the journey in a shorter time. Now, take that to the next step, where cars came into play and the few that could have a vehicle when they first came out could travel much quicker and much further. Now imagine all the people who were frightened at first by the automobile and did not trust to travel in one. It is a lot like that on our journey here on earth. When people were first introduced to Universal laws such as the law of attraction many many many years ago, most people thought it was crazy and would not work. Just like the automobile, after a time and seeing everyone who did have one seemed to be ok, the more open they were to the idea. Then people also felt safer to travel that way. Now, think of the airplane, can you imagine what people thought about that? Yet now most of the population of the planet uses it as transportation.

Now apply this concept to the spiritual awakening. It is like the tools we have now and with the consciousness on the planet. There were many great tools in the past to wake up and find true self, yet now that we can do it easier and quicker the old tools may not be the best to utilize at this time, much like people transitioning from using the horse to driving the car. They may use a horse for recreation now but they would not use a horse to go from one state to another. Then there are the ones who are the frequent flyers … like Oprah, who take the first leap. They were the first to take the plane and once everyone saw it was ok, now many will want to fly.

There will always be people who would rather walk, ride the horse, or drive the automobile and this is why the journey is so special. It is YOUR journey and you must travel it in the way you are most drawn. Either way, with accelerated consciousness on the planet at this time, everyone is moving more rapidly. We are in a time that is equivalent to flying in the plane opposed to taking the car. The Law of Attraction is happening more rapidly and this means that things are drawn to us like a magnet more quickly than before. If you have unresolved issues within you they will present them self more often and quicker than ever before. (More information on this later during this journey).

At the same time as we work on having a healthy life and connecting to our true authentic self, we are just as quickly drawing the wonderful things to us like a magnet. In my eighteen years of coaching people on transforming their life and in teaching workshops, I get a front seat view of these changes right before my eyes. I see the differences everyday in people's lives and what used to take a year for a client to work through within themselves, and change and move forward, is just matter of a two or three months.

This is a very exciting time. The more people who awaken and LIVE their true heart, the more that those people will want to give back by working with others on awakening. Can you imagine having a world where all are accountable for self, and in doing that assisting others on the planet to be accountable by teaching them how to create a happier life? It would spread like a wild fire and each small neighborhood at a time turns into a community and then a city, state, country and so on. However, before this can happen each one of us needs to wake up individually and then share the wisdom. I say wisdom because knowledge is knowing from reading it, being told about it, but wisdom comes from experience. We gain knowledge but unless we stretch out there and use that knowledge to see how it works for us, it is no more than words shared. However, when we take a risk in all cases and utilize (experience) that knowledge, we find out what works, what does not, or we add something and expand that knowledge to share, and this becomes wisdom.

Communication of the Deeper Heart

The consciousness awakening now on the planet is a deeper love, not the human perception of love. It is not love with conditions, or ifs, or judgments. This love is about realizing our connection no matter where someone is in his or her life. It is compassion and acceptance of everyone just as they are. It is not to be confused with thinking you have to be in places, situations, or issues with people with whom you have differences. It is to see them as they are, release them with love, and have no judgment. It is about being in deeper, more open, and honest relationships with others and ourselves. This happens through how we communicate. It is in being honest with ourselves about our feelings, communicating these feelings honestly and not defensively or guarded, being in integrity with self, and then radiating that out around us.

How do we get to this deeper heart? First, we must find our own heart. This means working through walls and barriers, the layers we spoke of earlier, and being truthful with ourselves about our own self. We need to FEEL our feelings and process through them. To process your feelings you cannot judge them but instead allow them to surface and learn to understand them and the reasons they have become a layer(s). Then when we have an understanding and know why we are experiencing them, we can make the transformation and express what we know and feel when needed. Be sensitive to others feelings and really FEEL what others are communicating, not just listen with the ears. Listen with your heart and feel their words. Interaction with others is what helps us to understand the interconnectedness we have with each other.

This may look simple on paper to you yet you may wonder why you feel you have such a difficult time actually FEELING your feelings, sharing them, and communicating them. Of course one of the obvious reasons is the many walls and barriers that we discussed earlier, that have been created from your life experiences going all the way back to when you were growing up; school, friends, parents, and relationships you have had.

It is not just our programs from childhood that have taught us to numb our feelings or to have difficulty in feeling and expressing them. Many times, it is our environment. We live in a faster paced world right now and ever growing. We have technology today that provides instant results and worldwide communications. These tools are teaching a different way to communicate. They also can be a distraction because of all the access we have to everything. Through much of this technology, we are able to research in front of a computer screen instead of a library where other people are. We can play games with the computer, or with people all over the world who are on the same game yet still have no eye contact or physical interaction. I do not think these are bad, if anything this technology has allowed us to hook up all over the world, meeting, sharing, and learning from people that we may have never been able to meet without the Internet.

Many times what we are not being aware of (mostly because it is so much of our NOW everyday life), how we are learning as a society to communicate. Most communications are through e-mail, cell phones, texts, and phone recorders. Cell phones have made our lives easier, especially with emergencies; recorders are invaluable. These are all great qualities and conveniences but as with everything in life, we must have balance. Anything used in excess is not a good thing.

Like every tool in the world, it is how we choose to use them. Many people have found it easier to communicate something uncomfortable in an e-mail, this way they do not have to be in front of the person and feel them, or let them see our body language and our expressions, which is a big part of communication. We avoid feelings, confrontations and so forth by leaving messages on recorders, texting instead of talking, and using the computer screen as an extra wall of protection.

Cell phones have taken us completely out of our now! You see almost every other car driving on the road and the driver is on the cell. People are talking on the phone while they shop, while they check out their groceries, and while they are out with other friends. When people are doing this on a regular basis, they have become on autopilot in their lives. Not to mention it is so dishonoring to the person you are having contact with in front of you, yes even the check out person.

The focus is not on the person's Now/present experience, and not being in the moment and less and less being aware of their surroundings. Most people have many great insights while driving, or they use the drive with some great music to unwind on the way home from somewhere. Now, if they get bored or lonely, or are avoiding being with themselves, they call someone on their cell phone. All of these tools can be distractions from paying attention and truly FEELING and walking IN your life, NOT just through your life.

Think about the newer generation growing up in this technology and learning from others to use these tools on a constant basis. If we do not teach these young ones balance in this technological world then their social skills will be lacking. The younger generation learn from what they see not what you say to them, learning from example. So when adults no longer consider it rude to be at the check stand and ignoring what is happening while having a conversation on the cell phone, then what are we teaching the younger ones? The one I love the most is when I see a couple or a family out for dinner and one or more of them HAS to answer their phone during the meal. Hmmm, and what ever happened to not being available at all moments of the day and at a whim? Before cell phones came along people talked to people they were with at the moment, so why is it people cannot just CHOOSE to not answer it.

Because of this technology, we have started to develop a completely new psychology around it. Now, if you do not answer your cell phone, people take it personal. They are convinced you just do not want to talk to them instead of thinking you are busy or just not in the mood to have the phone on. Then there is the Internet; you may feel one day while you are on the Internet that you want to get work done, so you block your name from everyone so you can work. Yet many Internet services have a feature that you can still check and see that a name is on line and just blocked and so people take it personal if they have checked to see if you are on and you are blocking. My thought would be, why are you even checking the name to see if it is on or blocked, because clearly, if you cannot see it on your buddy list, they do not want to be seen. Their ego tells them they are the only ones blocked on the list.

I teach Goddess weekends (women's retreat class) once a year and when I do, I rent beach houses and make sure no phones are at the houses, and usually in the areas I rent, the cell phones do not get a signal. It amazes me no matter how many different groups that I have, in every one of them someone will mention how grateful they are that their phone does not work. That always amazes me because they feel obligated to have it on and become justified at not having to answer it if they just do not get a signal. Again, this is so they do not have to communicate to people their needs or feelings. They have a hard time just saying, "I wanted private or alone time, so I turned my phone off," and that is even if you feel a need to explain your actions. It is as if the phone controls them instead of the phone being a tool they have control of by choices. I am not saying everyone is like this but if you look around there are a mass amount of people glued to their phones. The phone is a tool and you have control and choice with this tool on how to use it, how often and how it serves you in life. We have to be awake to make a choice of how we desire to use this tool in our life.

I do not think there is anything wrong with any of this great technology. The Internet and cell phone is a great asset and connects us to people all over the world we may have never met if not for these tools. I am saying we have to learn balance with them. How we use them is a reflection of how we communicate and interact in our daily lives.

More and more we will need to be more conscious of our heart and feelings, the shifts on the planet will urge and push at us until we do. The more we live in the higher energies of Oneness, the more we will feel the tug to open our hearts. Many on the planet relate an open heart to being open to hurt or to become vulnerable, or to love too much and then wish they had not. These old patterns are all based on experiences and past ideas of what love and an open heart really are. It is not what we learned growing up and if we choose today that it is not true in our life from this day forward then we will change that pattern. Many felt they loved at the risk of compromising themselves so much they lost who they really were. In fact, they really based who they were by being what others wanted or what they thought others wanted which is how they lost themselves.

The best way to learn about the true heart and the deeper communication of the heart is to find the real you in it first with no preconceptions of what that is or what others think it should be. The best way to start with this is to sit alone with self, and just FEEL! Let whatever comes up surface inside of you and do not judge or analyze it. The easiest way to open the heart is to first desire to do so and with the idea that it will be wonderful and not have a preconceived idea that it will lead to pain. Take baby steps, realize you really are learning to open the heart and it is something foreign to you. Be gentle with yourself when you walk through this process. You may want to start with a simple list of questions to get used to making choices about everything in your life moment to moment like: Do I want this for dinner? When you ask these questions really pay attention to how you feel inside when you answer them.

That may sound too simple but let me give you an example of the answers. If you choose baked chicken instead of deep fried chicken then this serves you in a physically healthy way. When we are healthy, we are healthier for the loved ones around us so it serves them in a healthy way also. Is it from love? Yes! Love of self and love for the ones around us.

Ask yourself these questions before you make a choice or take an action in your life.

Healthy means not compromising yourself and it is something that feels good inside of you.

> How does this serve/assist
> me in a healthy way?
> How does this serve/assist
> others in a healthy way?
> Is this coming from love?

Apply this exercise before every choice or action in your life and see how it may change many of your choices, or at least assist you in seeing them from a different perception.

To wake up we need to just move outside the box and have an understanding of how universal laws work. Just knowing of them will start the mind to think and explore possibilities. Pay attention to our God given senses, which are our internal voice and feelings. Remember we are mind, body, and spirit and so we listen, see and feel with all of our being: with our minds, our gut feelings, and our physical body. These are our own internal sensor to let us know what feels good to us and what is right for us. Above all, have fun doing it.

Exercises to Help Open Your Heart

You may want to begin with some and eventually do all of these exercises. You can ask for assistance with these exercises from the universe, Source, your guides or angels depending on your belief system.

1) Spend one day in your home with just yourself and have no contact with anyone in any form such as phone, e-mail, or text. Play music or just sit and write. Breathe and feel what comes up for you. Do you get antsy, frustrated, lonely, or bored? Keep a journal and write all things that come up. Pay attention to your body. See and feel if you are tense, fidgety and so forth? Do this a few times, a week or so apart, and note how things change. This will assist you to get more comfortable with staying with yourself.

2) Take a drive or a walk and be quiet inside and feel everything around you. Act as if you are feeling everything for the first time, with all new and fresh perceptions. On returning from your journey, write in your journal about how you perceived things and how you had different feelings. How did deep green feel to you or a gentle wind across your face? Be descriptive about these feelings. Explore different ways to describe what you feel by using sensations or use an experience. Example: The wind gently crossed my face and it made me feel warm and calm inside. I felt calm like the time I was on a sailboat drifting on a calm lake and was rocked gently by the water until I fell asleep.

3) Go shopping and walk around and let your self be drawn to things, maybe a whole new look in clothes. Work on really leaving the perceived you at home, the one that judges that you like those kind of clothes but not for you or on you. Just walk around and see what you are drawn to, pick new colors and styles and go try them on. Have fun with it knowing you are playing and exploring and you do not have to buy any of it. Again, on returning home write what you experienced and how you felt, even write on what it felt like to go out and explore. Was it hard for you to just go by yourself? Did you feel silly, happy, or uncomfortable?

4) As you get used to this, do something more stretching. Go to a party or a movie by yourself, or go somewhere and decide for the whole day you will smile at everyone you see, or talk to someone you do not know and note how it makes you feel inside.

5) Start paying attention to when you feel safer or more comfortable using the cell phone or the e-mail instead of seeing and facing someone. After recognizing it as avoidance, write what your worse fears are if you had to do it face to face.

6) Choose to turn your phones off for certain amounts of time during the day and again note how you feel.

7) Take two days and decide not to check e-mail or go on the computer.

8) Become aware of how many times in a day you leave your now, and what you are experiencing because you used the cell phone during your day out in the world. After being aware how often you do that, work on stopping yourself in the moment of your distraction and make a different choice in that moment.

These are all baby steps to start getting used to opening up. Of course, as you get more comfortable with it and you get deeper in the heart you will experience deeper and more profound experiences. As you open more, get to know the deeper heart of yourself, and then you can stretch out there, interact with others from the new you, and learn better and deeper ways to communicate with others. To get past fears of being yourself all the time, you need to get to the REAL you first in order to be the REAL YOU.

Have a heart felt experience with these exercises, be good and true to you.

NOW, write or draw How You FEEL right now.

Write down all your connections in the phones in your life right now. Then go back and put an "X" through the ones you feel are draining or unhealthy.

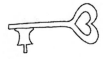

Keys to Wake from the Slumber

- Rules Inside of Our-Selves: What, Why and How to Break Them
- Recognize Programs; Is It Truth? Or a False Layer?
- Make New Choices with a New Perception for a True Heart
- Look Deep Inside Your Self

Wake from the Slumber

You may be wondering what I mean by falling asleep. I am referring to when you started to make rules inside yourself based on your life experiences instead of from your true heart. There are many examples. The first time you realized that saying certain things to adults were not ok, you made the rule, "don't share that again." The first time you realized about emotional hurt and decided not to feel that again. The first time you realized your parents wanted you to be a teacher instead of what your heart told you to be, which was a veterinarian, and so you pursued a road to be a teacher. Look for the first time you chose to ignore or shut out your true heart.

In sharing my own experience with this, when I was a child I always wanted to do work that helped others. I was always volunteering to stay after school and help the nuns put things away or help in the library. I was always bringing wounded birds home for my dad to fix and make better. I was constantly hearing from my father that I cannot save the world and I would not make a change. He believed that the world was how it was and getting worse and he felt my endeavors to help or heal were futile. My father instead encouraged me to do something beneficial that made money. I ended up working in computers for a corporation which I hated doing. Feeling at a loss of what I felt my true passion was I unconsciously started helping people by listening to their problems at break and lunch. I would seek solutions to their problems and share them with them. I also wanted to volunteer for different organizations and ended up a representative for United Way for a time. Somehow, within us we still remember the truth of who we are even if we have fallen asleep. It is still there and talking to us, nudging us back to our true self. However, as I became more of the corporate woman I was adding on layers of what I thought I should be doing in life. This self-created layer was assisting me in falling deeper into the sleep.

After we begin adding on these layers of thoughts and actions outside of our true hearts desires, we start to forget what they were; we might even have bought into the idea that our new thoughts were our own desires. As we journey on in this way, it starts to get complicated, for we forget who our true self is. Once we realize we are not feeling happy and peaceful inside, we really do not know why.

We then feel at a loss as to how to feel happy, or what it would take to feel this happiness and peacefulness. The answer is to start removing all those false layers we accumulated and as we do, we will start to get back in touch with our true heart by waking from the slumber. The thing is though, as we remove the other false and unhealthy layers we start to hear our ego voices, judgments about what we are doing. We experience judgments from family or friends who knew our false self and had become comfortable with that part of us. They are unsure about the changes that are occurring in us and they are not sure how to deal with the new us, which in reality is our true self.

How do we discover our true self? How do we find out what our false selves and old programs are?

There are many ways to do this. One way is to go back in your mind and remember things you loved to do, things you always felt drawn to when you were little. Was it art? Was it a deep love and connection with animals? Take the things you loved to do and ask yourself now if you still feel drawn to them, yet gave up the dream because someone commented that you would never be able to do that, or you would never make good money at it. When you ask yourself now if this is something that still peaks your inner passion, pay attention not only to the answer in your head, pay attention to how you feel emotionally when you ask it, and how your physical body feels. Note if it is excited, or bottoms out, see if your body gets tense, and pay attention to all of your senses.

Another way to find other old programs is to pay attention to what you say to yourself on a regular basis. For example, are you always thinking you are not good enough, cannot do things perfect enough, or are not deserving of wonderful things in your life? How do you feel about your looks? Are you confident in your choices?

Look at actions you take in your life. Such as, are you someone who gives so much to others you never have time for you? Yes, this comes from an old program. Do you pride yourself in how much you can do and handle on your own and refuse help from others? Look at the relationships you have, are they healthy relationships? Do your friends count on you for everything; or are they balanced in giving and receiving? Do you enjoy being with all of the people that you call friends? Have you had or have a healthy intimate relationship? All of these things will let you know where you have old programs left inside to work out.

Since we took on the rules that are from our old programs, we now have been basing our choices in life on these programs and may not even be aware of it anymore. One of my clients had a mother she felt was very negative as a mom, so she made the rule she would never be like her. From that simple rule, this is what occurred: her mom never spent time with her; she never listened, and just dictated to her. Her mother never went to school functions, and her mom was all about herself. This woman, who experienced this as the daughter, after making her rule never to be like her mom, spent the rest of her life trying to be super mom. Now, it is good to be an attentive nurturing and loving mom, but this woman went overboard with it. To be that good mom, she overachieved by joining too many committees at school, over extending herself to the detriment of her own health and emotional well-being. She mothered everyone and left little time to take care of herself. As she was making these choices to be all to everyone, she no longer realized it came from that one rule she made, that she would not be like her mom. On some subconscious level, she was constantly proving to herself she was not like her mother by trying to be a perfect mother to everyone. She based all these choices in her life off that one rule she made at twelve years old.

I had a male client who had a very passive father and a dominant mother. He watched his father on many occasions just sit quietly and not speak up for the children or himself. Without knowing that this was being programmed in his subconscious mind, he struggled through life not understanding why he kept choosing relationships with women who were dominant. Not only dominant but in an unhealthy manner, where he was suppressing his feelings and becoming like his father by doing whatever this person wanted at his own compromise. As I worked with him on this issue, he found that he also saw where it taught him never to be confrontational and in trying hard not to have confrontation, he would constantly stifle himself and suppress his feelings.

Another example was a client I had who had serious issues with men. She never trusted anyone especially men. She felt she had to do everything herself and swore she never needed the help of a man. Throughout her life, when she met healthy helpful men who did want to assist her in a healthy way, she would not allow herself to receive that help, thinking it meant she was breaking a rule of hers and it meant she could not do it herself. She would not let men too close to her in the heart, in fear that if she did she would always be hurt. She now was unconsciously making all these choices in her life based on when she was eleven years old and saw her dad was a liar and was hurtful to her mother. Her mother was trusting and verbalized often afterwards as she was growing up, that she was stupid to trust her father, and that she should have never been there and opened her heart so much to him, and then she would not have been so hurt. She was dependant on the father and also verbalized in front of my client several times, she did not know how she was going to make it now without a husband. The little girl hearing and seeing all of this, had created a rule in her mind, she would never love like that, never open her heart all the way, and never need a man. See how this affected her choices for the rest of her life?

After we heal these programs, we have to see how every choice in life that comes along is another door of opportunity that we can choose to be, feel, and make healthier choices in every given moment. Make new choices based on the true self and not the fearful child self, who made up protective rules. Those rules served their purpose when they were created but as we grow and heal, we realize using these rules of protection from hurt, is really an illusion. In actuality, these rules end up being our limitations and the actions will reap less joyful results in our lives.

If our hearts are closed or guarded, we are guarded in both directions, meaning we also do not let the full experience of love, joy, and peace in either. We cannot truly and fully love another with all of our hearts if our hearts are in dis-ease. How could we? A blocked heart has no concept of full love and joy, and even though we feel we are giving that out, we are not giving our whole heart out to others, because we cannot even know how to be a wholehearted person with these blocks.

After you are aware of the areas in which you still have old programs and patterns that are not reflecting your true heart, you can make choices to change and heal them. This will allow you to move forward to a happier life and one that your true heart is creating. All old programs need to be healed by viewing them, but you view them just to gain understanding of them, which helps you to heal and grow from them. It is always good to process them, but do not become addicted to the process. Many can get into healing the inner self and become process junkies, which can put you in a loop and not create true healing and growth. So view the areas you made these rules and why you made them or how you developed a certain self-image, then learn from them, why, and make a new choice on steps to take to heal and move into the true heart.

Beginning of the healing process

Many people may feel overwhelmed when they see how many areas in which they have not been their true selves. It does not have to be overwhelming, you can make a list of areas you want to change and then write which ones are affecting you and your life the most right in this moment. Take those and then commit to take steps to start working on them. Yes, I say take steps-baby steps and then you truly will heal the issue. When we try to jump from step one to ten, we always end up having to go back and take steps two through nine. Healing is a process. The best way to heal a situation inside is to go straight to the core. The core would be the very first time you made a rule, or made a judgment on yourself. Processing to every event back to the root, takes you back through much pain you do not need to walk through. If you go to the root of it, it unravels everything with understanding that has occurred after that moment into your now. It does not mean you will feel the pain of the first time, and then have sadness of all the following ones, but if you go back step-by-step to the first time, it creates experiences that are more painful each time you view it until you get to the root. Again, over processing can lead to becoming addicted to the process.

Once you have started to awaken to your true heart, you make decisions that are healthier for you. Many people will react around you, especially if you were the over giver and are now wanting time for you. Many will also be happy for you and support you in your growth and change. Whenever you take a leap and choose to better yourself, you provide an opportunity for the ones around you to work on their inner issues and grow. The key here is that they have an opportunity to "choose" to also grow and be happy. If they do not make that choice at this time, you may find yourself outgrowing people who were close to you. Others may choose to grow allowing you to have an even more rich and rewarding relationship with them.

The most important thing to remember when you start this journey of healing is to not beat yourself up. For many people, once they can see their past from an awake perception, they get angry they stayed in it so long. They start beating themselves up and thinking they should have seen it sooner. We all see things when we are ready to, there is no right or wrong to it. No one has a deadline in the universe to wake up or else. Remember when you look back, you were seeing the experience from the person you were then, and your created perceptions you acquired while walking the journey to that point. Instead, see that every experience, good or painful, was a message on the journey. It was giving you an opportunity each time for a lesson, and when we learn the lesson, we do not need to repeat it. It can also mean you learned a layer of the lessons, just not all the way to the root of the lesson. If we find ourselves repeating a lesson, we ask ourselves inside, what is it I still need to learn about this situation so I can complete and find peace with this lesson?

I always tell my clients, if you are repeating a lesson, do not get angry at it. Just because you are visiting it again does not mean you cannot make a different choice right then, in your now. Make a new choice that will assist you to complete the lesson. Many times, I have my clients step back from the situation and look at it from a distance, meaning a perspective that is not emotionally charged. Look at it, and look at the choices you may have in the situation, then weigh them and ask yourself is this more Joyful or less joyful … for me? Now, you may think that seems funny because you would assume that all people would always choose the more joyful. However, many times in my work, I have seen people know that a certain choice would be less joyful for them, yet they choose it anyway for many different reasons. It may be that they feel they are making it more joyful for another if they take the less joyful for themselves. Or they truly need to experience the lowest point to make a choice for change. This all comes down to loving yourself.

Do not be too hard on yourself with repeating lessons. Many a time when it means working down through the layers of pain or experiences, remember it took you a lifetime to where you are now, to build those layers. You are not going to just wake up and the layers have disappeared. That would be nice, but it just does not happen that way. If it did, we would all be healed and Masters of our Life. However, we are actually Masters in training in our life, so be gentle with yourself, and walk through the layers of understanding your true heart. There will be times, you will know, you must look deeper. We go down in our feelings and heart at the rate we feel we can handle at that given moment. So, sometimes we repeat things to keep working down through each layer and each time we grow, we can handle more and go deeper. Trust me, I know this feeling. At times in my life where I thought I had to be at the core, and then one of my teachers would say, go deeper, I used to think I would explode if I heard him say that one more time. But through my determination for wanting to understand myself and the world around me, to be happier in life, I was glad I never quit and I went deeper.

There are times you will repeat a scenario and it is not because you are repeating a lesson, instead it is to see if you are certain you are done with the old and you are ready for the new. Many times after reaching the core of the lesson, we may have it return to visit three times. Once to ask, do you think you are done with that? Twice, are sure you are done with that? The third time asking are you certain you are done with that? Most times this is the reason we are revisited. The good news is, once we are certain, there is no reason for it to visit us again.

I had many great teachers in my life, but one of them once said to me, you cannot give anything to someone you do not first own within yourself. Therefore, learning to love you first is the key to being able to truly love someone else from the true heart. Many times loving from your true heart and assisting someone is to say no to someone. We think if we are always helping or bailing someone out of a situation we are helping, when in fact all we are doing is helping him or her stay the way they are. We are assisting them to stay UN empowered. So next time you have any situation in life, step back, in your mind see a fork in the road and ask yourself, more joyful, less joyful, which path do I choose?

When we ask ourselves this question, we can use just our minds and think rationally about which is the more joyful path, but it is just as important to use our intuition and our inner voice.

Make a list of all the things you loved as a child.

Keys to Emotional Chords

- Memories, Emotions, Layers, and Transformation
- Acknowledge and Make Different Choices
- Obstacles as Opportunities
- Being not Doing
- Attention, Intention, Create
- How You Feel About Yourself
- Choose Joyful Living
- You Are Your First Priority

Emotional Chords

Emotional Chords is a term for a place inside of us that can be triggered by a word, an action, or even a smell. It is a place that is inside of us that reacts because of a previous experience or triggers a memory. We may not be consciously aware of all chords or why and what they are attached to. We can have joyful chords or less joyful ones and it is the less joyful ones we want to work on and heal. One of my more joyful chords is the smell of pies cooking. I automatically smile and have wonderful memories of my sister Kathy and I baking together and laughing as we did. A less joyful chord of mine used to be that every time I smelled the cologne Brute I would feel angry and actually did not know why. Many years after experiencing this, I learned through my self-journey work that I was beat up by a young man when I was twelve years old, and he smelled strongly of Brute cologne. Now, I did not remember the beating when I smelled the Brute at that moment, yet it would push an emotional button inside me where this memory was stuck. This is why part of the journey is to uncover memories inside of us that are stuck so we can acknowledge them and heal them. We want to transform these memories though and not get stuck on the working on them part.

When we are working on our past and the chords/memories we want to transform, many people become stuck and addicted to the processing. Why? Maybe they feel they do not have any tools to move out of it, or maybe they are in fear of moving into the new, because at that time, it is the unknown to them. If your life has been trauma and drama for a long time then it is hard to conceive of it being joyful, calm, and loving. But it CAN! We just need to recognize our chords, our emotionally charged points, and then know why we have them and make a choice that we want to transform them. If you wallow in the feeling that comes up it will slow or prevent you from walking through them. When we view a past event, it is ok to feel it, and then see it for what it is teaching us and then release it. Many of the old therapies, which were good for back then, taught to ponder it for days. Write on it, feel it many times. I felt it seemed I was being told to regurgitate it. I learned from once again a wise teacher in my life, why bring this energy into your now and then hold it here in your now? Didn't you experience the hurt of it already and live in the trauma of it already? You just need to view the lessons, not be stuck in the trauma drama of it again. Was it not enough for you when you walked through it? All of these points were good points, and very thought provoking. When I started asking myself these questions, I saw the wisdom of just viewing, learning the lesson, and releasing it.

When I have a client that decides to stay in their past pain, which is actually making it a part of their present life, I have them take a piece of meat and call it their pain. Then I tell them to chop it up and ask, is it still steak? Yes! Ok, now let us pound it flat, is it still steak? Yes! Ok, then I have them throw it in the food processor, and ask, is it still steak? Yes! I then point out, you can take that pain from the past, bring it forward and chop it, bang it, process it until it is beaten to death, but it is still the same pain. Only now you choose to hang on to it, bring it in your now and over process something you already experienced. How is that exactly working for you?

If you want to heal inside and move forward, you must transform these past hurts by seeing them as teachers and a lesson presented to you for growth. Not to be stuck in them and relive it over and over. One client I had, no matter how many tools I gave her, or how many opportunities I assisted with guiding to ways to move through something, she would find a reason to hang on and go back to the pain. I finally told her to tell me every significant time that came up in her life that made an impact on her. She named every single painful tragedy (in her perception) that she experienced. I then told her to tell me all the pivotal moments in just the last two years, and it was no different. I then told her, to give me a call when she had had enough and really wanted to move forward. Remember, to transform our lives, to use all our life experiences as tools and lessons, and what made us who we are today, is all a choice. We choose who we are today.

Transforming old programs is about changing your perception. Change how you view them, and instead of treating them as obstacles see them as opportunities. Opportunities you can learn from.

A good exercise is to list some of the many thoughts, behaviors, or habits you notice you have every day.

Examples:

Your relationship with food, do you over eat or don't eat healthy as in five times a day?

Do you gossip about others?

Do you tend to drink when stressed?

Are you judgmental or critical of self or others?

Do you compare yourself to others?

Do you not speak your feelings or truth and instead let them buildup until you feel resentment?

Do you often tell stories that always make you the victim?

Do you always follow someone else's good news or story with a better one of your own?

List some of the many thoughts, behaviors, or habits you notice you have every day.

The next step is to look at what causes you to make unhealthy choices. We think it is an outside person or event that is causing us to react this way. In reality, we choose whom we hang out with or what events we choose to be around. Our choices seem so automatic or so habitual, maybe based on past experiences that we are no longer conscious we are still making a choice in that moment. The truth is, in every given moment we are choosing to BE in the state we are finding our self in. We have the choice of how we want to feel and how we want to act, not react.

Let us take the list of examples above and ask yourself for any of the ones you chose,

How does this serve me?	How is it making me feel inside?

If you chose gossip about others, you may look at how that serves you. Do you feel it makes you popular or that it makes you stand out to know something about another? Is it making you feel important in some way?

The next step is to recognize this is unhealthy behavior and so is taking the less joyful path. You then can choose to make a different path in life. Next time you are about to gossip realize in your mind how it was serving you and choose not to gossip. Then find a new way you can love yourself by just being yourself and not needing to gossip for the illusion of self-importance.

The key to changing these programs is to look at your journey so far, and then look at what you would like your journey to truly be. Choose what experiences you want on the path of your journey. Less joyful, more joyful? That is the question. To be your authentic self, your TRUE heart, you have to look at each situation, and even if it hits an old chord choose a different way to see it, and choose to act on it, not react.

Actively Live Your Life

Your life is the journey and you can live it consciously by being aware of choices in the moment, which is BEING life, or you can numbly make choices and be DOING life. Truly living and BEING life is knowing that you have freedom of choice and you are accountable for your own choices in life. To live and BE our life means we know we can make better choices every moment we breathe. It is like when I am teaching or dancing, I am not doing teaching or dancing, it comes from my true heart, so I am being my teaching or dancing, I am expressing my inner self. A full expression of the true me inside, and if I own the true me, I can only BE, NOT DO.

An example of where I felt at a time in my life I was doing instead of being was when I was growing up. I grew up Catholic and went to Catholic school. I just assumed as a young child, I just WAS Catholic, because I was told I was and I went to Catholic school. Then one day in fourth grade I heard one of my school teachers say, we are practicing Catholics. Well, my mind thought, how could I be practicing how to be a Catholic, I either am or not? That term always bothered me. The good news is I had the AHA moment that said, if I am practicing it, I am not it yet, so I wonder if I want to be it. My mind related it to taking piano lessons, I was not a piano player yet I was practicing to play and could become a piano player but it did not mean for sure I would be one. This sent me on another part of my journey, which led me to explore other religions and see what I wanted to be. My point here is, if I truly inside myself had felt I was a Catholic and embraced all of it, I would not have had the need to explore elsewhere, yet I am very glad I did. I did not own inside myself I was a Catholic and always felt that way, but when hearing that statement, it opened a door and gave me an opportunity to examine myself and make a different choice. I so love all the AHA moments in life, they are such great catalysts. Whatever motivates you is great; just get motivated to make new choices in life.

How do we start living this way?

You choose it, and how you are choosing to live your life goes back to how energy/ thoughts work, where my attention is my intention is. You consciously put your attention on the Owning it inside, and how you want your journey to look and feel, how you want it to BE. If you know you want happiness, love, and peace, then you will make new choices that bring that to you, and let go of all that does not reflect that.

I hear so many of my clients say, they are not happy in their relationship, or their jobs, and my question to them is, then why are you in them? Sounds simple, but many think well, I have to make money, well, I cannot hurt that person so I stay, or I do not know what I would do alone. Many jobs pay money, why not find one you enjoy more? If you are already unhappy being with someone, why not be on your own and learn to create your own happiness? What is really happening, is that these people are staying in the old programs of I can't be happy, victim role, or life is hard. It is all a choice. It is where you put your attention that your intention is!

If you focus your attention on hurt, lack of abundance, your intention is sending that out and calling it back into your life. If your attention is on peace, love, joy, and happiness, then that is your intention and it will come to you. Again, you must CHOOSE these things.

When we ignore things in life, we really end up doing them. Making them occur. A good example, I at one time in my life always forgot to eat. What was really happening was, my body would be hungry and my stomach would growl, but I was busy so I just kept ignoring it. Soon, I no longer FELT hungry, so became NOT hungry. I put my attention on my work to forget I was hungry, but that sent the intention, I am not hungry out there and it became so. This of course was not healthy for my body. Like anything else in life, this is what will happen. If you ignore that you dislike your job and your attention is to just cope with it and settle for it, or your thoughts are I will not find anything better, then this is how the energy will return. You will not be able to find a new and better job and you will manifest situations to validate you need to stay and settle for the job you are in. The result is, settling for less than and not finding a better job.

Be conscious and aware as much as you can during the day to what your attention is on. Close your eyes every morning, take a few relaxing breaths and then see your day with your intention for the day. It could be, I will make new friends today, I will be abundant in all I do today, and I will have new opportunities today. Then feel inside what a day like that would make you feel like. Feel the joy and love inside of you, and see how long you can keep these feelings and intentions going. Even if at first it is only fifteen minutes, keep being this feeling and thought, bring yourself back to it every time you slip out of it, pretty soon you will notice that your attention is mostly on what you really want, the true heart.

To transform these habits and automatic doing in your life, take the list you made earlier, like the gossiping, relationship to food, and so forth and make a new list. For instance, if you said gossiping, instead write on the list, I see the highest good or potential in others. Take I do not speak my truths until I have held in my feelings long enough to build up resentment, and instead write, I always lovingly speak my true feelings in every moment and create healthy communications and relationships. Do this for all the habits you wrote down earlier, and now carry around just this new list. Make this list what you work with for putting your attention on during the day. The more you shift your attention, the more you will start to see things, situations, and people in a new way. It will assist you to shift your perceptions on life.

You can list here while you are thinking about it but be sure to list on another sheet of paper so that you can carry it with you to help you focus your attention.

Each one of the following sentences has an emotional charge chord to it.
I never have enough money.
I never have enough time in the day.
I try hard to change and be happy, but it just does not work for me.
I never get my needs met.
It is my friends, co-workers, or families fault I am like this.
I never feel good enough.
If I just had a helpful mate.
If I just had more_____.

It is not any of these things that will bring you happiness or peace. Putting your attention on them daily will continue to create circumstances in your life to validate that these statements are true. All of those sentences came from a program. It could have been your mom or dad always said we never have enough. If you feel you never get your needs met, it could be because you are too busy being the over giver to everyone else. Point is you are choosing this. The more you have these thoughts the more you sink into the pity pot and nothing good ever comes out of that pot.

Make a choice to change it, and write steps you are willing to take every day to make that change. One of the common things I hear from some clients, is I haven't enough time to work on me, or I can't stop being an over giver right now, too many people depend on me. These are all excuses for not wanting to truly face your programs and question your rules. It is fear! I tell my clients to name something small or large they wanted bad in life, and swore they would get it. It could be a dress, a concert, or a trip. Most people will swear how broke they are, yet will manage to get that dress, that concert ticket, or that trip. Why? Because they really wanted it! So, you have to ask yourself honestly, how much do you truly want to be happy, abundant, calm, free of drama, and LIVE life fully? If you find you still cannot get out of the pity pot, do this. Get a tape recorder and tell your pity story over and over for one hour. Tell it like you would tell it to a best friend. Go on and on about how bad things are and all the reasons why you cannot change it. Then take this tape and ear phones and listen to it over and over again until you just cannot stand the story anymore. When you get to this point, you are ready to truly want a new and happier life, so now destroy the tape.

Those types of negative thoughts about self are self-sabotaging. If you stay in the negative thought patterns, you are abusing yourself because you are beating your own self and self-esteem up. It is easy to say just dismiss them, yet it feels more difficult when you have had them for so long about yourself. Think about it like this, if you were around a person who constantly speaks negatively or someone being verbally abusive, you would walk away from them, correct? At least I hope this is the case. Just as you would not allow those negative actions of people to be in your space, just DO NOT allow those same negative thoughts of yours around you any longer. It really does not have to be hard or difficult; it can be as simple as CHOOSE differently!

Once your attention is on the true heart and the desire to have a happy life, choose one step to BE all week that will bring you closer to what you truly want. Be creative, if you want to feel better about yourself, then every morning tell yourself how beautiful and deserving you are. Dress the way you want to feel about yourself. You will not allow greatness into your life if you do not love yourself and feel you are worth it and deserving. You must be in a place of receiving without guilt. If you were looking at yourself through the eyes of soul, and seeing your true heart, there is nothing there NOT to love. If you see any part of yourself that you do not love, then that is not your true heart, it is programs that you acquired and are living out in life. If you are still having a tough time with this, get that great tape recorder out again, and talk for one hour on how wonderful you are. Tell yourself all the great qualities you have, all your talents, everything of the true heart. Talk to the tape as if it were a best friend or an angel telling you about you. How you have a beautiful smile, sparkling eyes, and great love for others and so on. Talk a full hour telling yourself what an angel would tell you about you. Then play this tape every day, more than once, until you own it and you feel it, and your attention is on your wonderful self. Each exercise you do, is taking the attention into action. Make action steps every day, until you feel and know a difference in yourself.

When I say BE or being, I mean that what you truly want comes from your heart and soul and you want to walk in that all day. This does not mean THINGS such as monetary or outcomes of a sort. I mean experienced feelings. Many people believe to have what they deserve it is 'things', and then when they have them they are still not fulfilled and happy. So, what I mean by BEING is being your soul. Knowing the minute that you were born and entered that body, you were loving, loved, valuable and meaningful. It is how we choose to walk our life that makes it whether we know this and walk it or not. If you believe you are a victim, you will stay a victim. There is a time in your life when you have to make a choice to no longer be a victim and empower yourself, for no one else can empower you for you. Only you can, take a stance and take action. Things are tools, and they are reflections of what we own inside about ourselves. So if you are abundant in love and rich in experience, which is wisdom, then yes, you probably will also have many wonderful things in your life, it is law of attraction. Like attracts like. Negative thoughts and feelings about yourself will draw negative situations to you and lack.

Be conscious of what your attention is on and look at how on the subtler levels you may be attracting what you have in your life now. If you have based an intention on an emotional need, many times this is not what you truly wanted from the true heart. An example would be someone who is feeling very lonely might put intention on having a man or woman in his or her life to fill that void. Emotionally you may feel clear that this is what you want, but if you are asking for this out of the need to fill a void you will not attract what your true heart is wanting. The emotionally charged part of you is sending signals out to attract a person to fill the void. The true heart is looking for self-love and to be loved and share the journey with a partner to grow and be joyful with. If your emotional self is attracting the intention of just fill the void, you may call relationships in that are unfulfilling, but you are no longer alone. See what I mean?

Tools you can use when you feel stuck in a negative thought pattern:

Write whatever comes to your mind, continually sit there with the pen and paper, and just write all that is coming to you. Once it is all out, burn it or release it in some way that feels comfortable to you.

Write anything you feel inside that you have always felt could never be spoken. Any feelings at all that you feel, but would never speak to a person about. Also burn and release.

If you really feel stuck on a worry or fear, then write it down. Then write out a scenario that is the worst possible thing you can think of that could happen from this worry or fear. Write it in the worst way you can think of it happening. Then go back and read it, acting as if this has already happened to you. Once you do this, if all this had happened to you what would you have learned from it? Let me show you an example and then show you what to do with it:

Worry or fear: Not having enough money to live well.

Worst that could happen: My utilities would be turned off and my kids would suffer. I would lose my house and be on the street. I would have no way to get to work and I would be without all my furnishings. I would be with my kids all the time but have nowhere for them to live properly and take care of them.

Lessons: I learned to be grateful for having a place to live, for having the luxuries of utilities. I learned I can be a good parent even without a place to live, to have quality time with my children, and that our love was stronger when we were all together in this. I learned other resources of making money and still being there for my children. I learned to receive because I allowed others to help me when I had no place to live. I learned to be humble. I learned about others genuine love and support, and compassion.

Worst Case Scenario
Worry or Fear:
Worst thing that could happen:

Lessons:

Now, take this list of lessons and know that these are lessons you need to learn. If you start working on these lessons and learn them the way you are living now, then there is no need to live the worst thing that could happen. It is about learning the lessons and how you choose to learn them, less joyful path, most joyful path?

Pay Attention, the Universe is Talking

I tell my students in my class, this is the way the universe talks to us, and of course, this is the way our inner self calls things to us. First, the universe whispers to us, then if we do not get the message/lesson, then the universe talks in a regular voice, if we still do not get it, then it yells louder, and if we still do not get it, we get a baseball bat across our head (nerf bat).

Example: We hear a whisper we do not like our job and should look for a different one. We do not, so our jobs become worse, hard to deal with and yet we still stay there. So now, our job is so bad we are drained of energy, we hate getting up and going in and anticipate it to be bad before getting there. Now, the universal baseball bat comes and we are laid off or fired, and now we have to find another job. Hmmm, less joyful path people. So, does the lesson end here, no! Now we have a choice, we can go and find a job just as horrible so we can validate our bad story on how work sucks or we can choose to hold out and wait and find the job we really want and feel happy at. The more joyful path is to listen to the messages when they are still whispers or normal tone.

You Are Worth It

To do this, you must be awake and pay attention to the messages. First, you must learn to start loving you and feeling worthy to accept and receive messages of love and joy. How can we hear messages that we deserve happiness and how can we get there if we are feeling we do not deserve them? You are not going to hear your higher self telling you to go for that great wonderful loving relationship if you feel you are not worth it.

Do this by looking at all the thoughts you have about yourself daily. How many times do you get a compliment and down play it instead of just saying thank you? Do you say things like I am not good enough, I am stupid, clumsy, or compare yourself to someone else by saying things like, oh s/he does it better? Take a little notebook around with you and every time you criticize yourself, or down play a compliment or have a negative thought about yourself, write it down. Then when you have time to yourself, look at this list, and ask why you feel or think these ways. Were they just programs from what you heard growing up? Did you develop them later and if so why? You have to know in your true heart these are not truths about yourself, but if you bought into them at one time as truth, you may have become some of them. Either way, they are not your true heart self, so choose to change your perception and any actions you do that no longer serve you in a healthy and happy life. Start to see the true you, the desired you, the lovable and loving you.

In loving our self, it is not just changing our perception but taking action by doing things in our lives that make us know we are worth it. When you get it and you own it, you will BE it. Once we are BEING our true authentic heart we will not allow anything dishonoring to us in our life.

What do I mean by that? Well, if we did not love our self we probably were allowing disrespectful behavior toward us. If we are someone who gives too much of ourselves to everyone, then many who were used to us being that way might have started to take advantage of that by dumping an enormous amount of weight on us. Now, you need to see your accountability in these situations. If you are someone who gave to everyone else at the compromise of yourself, which is usually subconsciously done to make you feel better about yourself, than most likely you had a program that told you "I am never good enough." This is how you became (chose) to give too much and then you taught the ones around you that they could take advantage the very first time they dumped your way and you did not say NO or that is not okay. Okay, so you are accountable for that but it does not mean you cannot change your way, grow and decide this is not the way you want to live anymore. So, now you learn about having boundaries, saying no, honoring yourself, and in return others will start to honor you too. If we had no boundaries, no self-respect and we did not have enough self-love for us not to be used, why would someone else have that respect and honor for us? They wouldn't. You might say, but I have always done this, so no one will understand and they will be mad at me or not like me. Well, this could be true, but they will get over it. If you openly speak your heart and say, I know I used to do this but I am working on loving myself and taking steps to heal my heart, so I now have boundaries, healthy for me boundaries. The people in your life can learn and grow with you and support you in this healthy change, or they can choose to stay how they are and you will outgrow them. The great thing is, we all have a choice, and we are not responsible for another's choice nor are we responsible for the journey they choose for themselves.

Honor and respect you, nurture and love you, take special pampering time for you with NO guilt, and you will receive the same from others. Be brave and take a stand, it may help another person see how it works for you and inspire them to heal themselves too.

Pamper yourself with one small thing a day to start with. Make a list at the end of this chapter of ways you could do this. Here are some examples:

Take a hot bubble bath with candles and no distractions.
Buy yourself beautiful flowers.
Take yourself or a friend to a great fancy restaurant.
Work yourself up with tiny steps and then branch out and go from there.

Tools and ideas to start with to nurture and love you:

Physical nurturing: Get an exercise that is fun; belly dancing, riding a bike, walking in a nearby treesy area, swim, take bubble baths and add bath paints, make it fun.

Emotional nurturing: Invite friends over to laugh, play board games, do make believe fantasy readings, dance, garden, start a fairy corner, blow bubbles.

Spiritual nurturing: Make or decorate a journal, have a party full of games anytime. Have a passion party, call the muses, and get ideas for creativity. You can start with the party planner at the end of this chapter. Make and decorate an altar to reflect your spiritual journey and to honor you, add play and joy. Start a silly journal where you can be characters, create characters, or just be silly.

Be creative and do not judge anything you want to do to make more joy in your life.

A LETTER FROM MY ANGEL

Take a few deep breaths and let go of any tension you feel. Sit down with a pen and paper (you may copy the next page) and just relax. Now, close your eyes for a moment, and just think of something that makes you feel good, something that makes you feel as if you are in your heart and feeling warm inside. Now decide you will write yourself a letter from your angels and it will be all about you. If an angel were to write you a letter all about you, what would they say? See you through the eyes of the angel and start writing. Do not stop or think about it, just keep writing until you feel done and have told you all you would say and see if you were an angel. When you have finished this letter, do not read it, put it in an envelope, address it to yourself, and put a stamp on it. In three days, mail it to yourself. Trust me on this. When you receive it, then sit down and read it as if hearing it for the first time.

Write a letter to yourself as if your angel was writing to you about you, through angel's eyes.

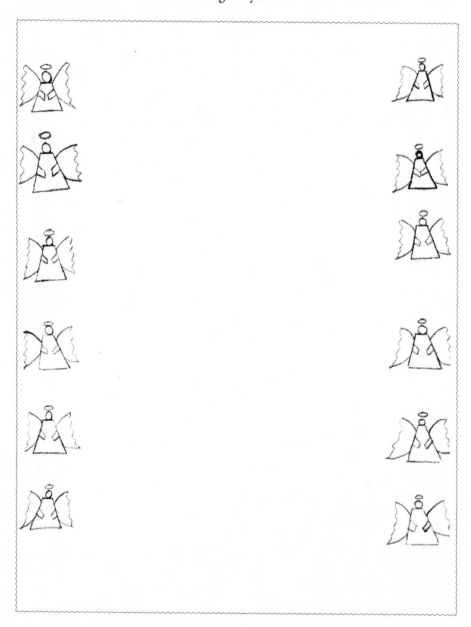

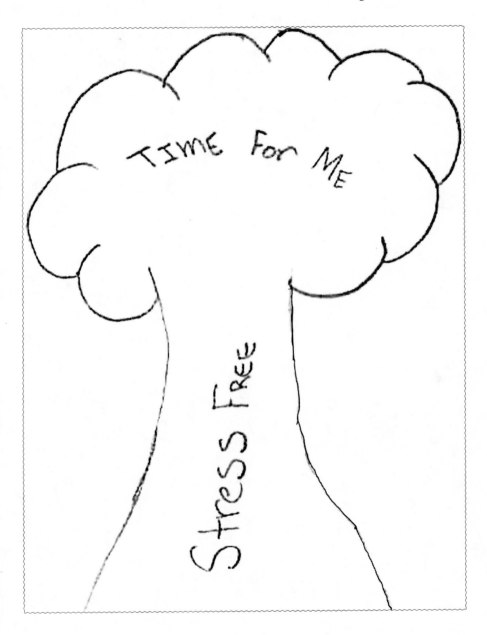

Write a list of things you can do this week to pamper yourself. You can put things like bubble bath, candlelight and quiet time and so forth. After making the list do as many as you can this week for yourself.

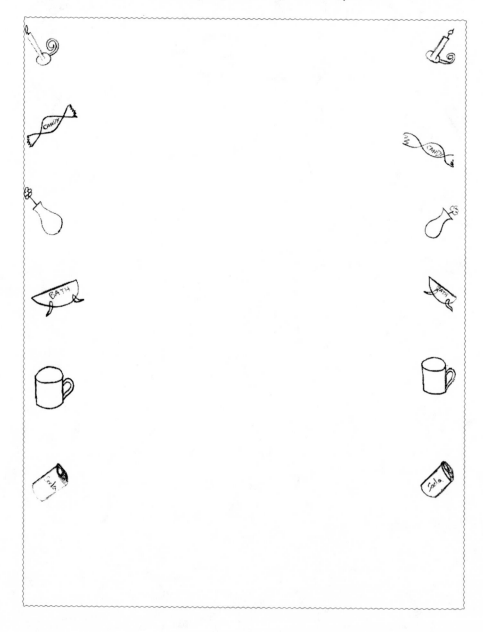

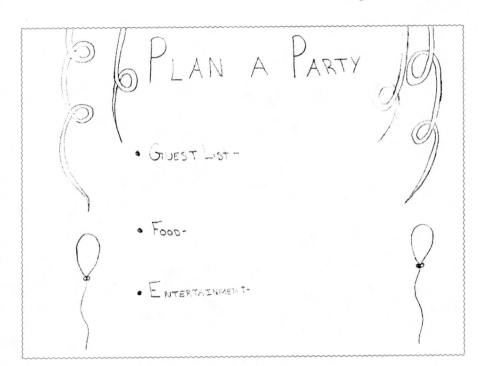

PLAN A PARTY

- GUEST LIST -

- FOOD -

- ENTERTAINMENT -

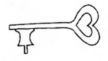

Keys to Fears

- Rules Based on Fears We Created to Protect Our Self
- Be In the Moment
- How Can I See Things from a Better/Different Perspective?
- Don't Let Fear Make Your Choices
- Acknowledge, Heal, and Let Go of Your Past
- Take Lessons Learned in Life and Move Forward
- Ask Yourself Why You Are Choosing the Experiences in Your Present Moment
- Give Ego a New Job to Do

Fears

Fears are the root of every program/rule we created and the root of what our ego voice warns us about. Whatever rules we created, we created to protect ourselves to survive on some level, whether it is emotional, physical, or mental. To survive or to want protection means we fear something such as getting hurt, trusting, and being betrayed and so forth. Fear can influence our want to grow and change. If we recognize we want to change our life and heal our past, fear will also warn us NOT to go back in our past. Fear thinks it is protecting us from having to review our pain and wounds. I won't say it is a breeze to choose to walk the path of awareness; it does take courage to look at our life, our fears, work through them, and be accountable that we create our reality. This means if we are still running an old rule we are living in fear of something and it is dictating and controlling the choices we make in our life. The good news is, once you do the work, you are working only on moving forward and in a happier and more fulfilling life.

Fear pushes us to make decisions based on reaction, instead of action. We consciously and unconsciously believe that our rules are protection from manifesting our deepest fears when in reality our fear is limiting. It keeps us from taking a leap of faith, trusting our inner higher self, and having happy situations in our lives. We validate our fears by saying to ourselves that it has helped us in the past. But, it isn't our rules or fears that create what we experience, unless all you run is fear. We create our experiences in life by what we have as core beliefs. If your core belief is that you deserve a happy trusting relationship, then that is what you will get. Where if you fear always being wrong about love and the people you choose to love, and fear always to be hurt, then this is what you will create and experience.

Your past is what caused you to make the choices of making rules based on fears. You must move forward from your rules and break them loose, take a risk, trust and BE/ACT instead of listening to the woes of fear and reacting. You cannot move into your future if your past is constantly in your present. If you were experiencing hurt or loss in your past, then look at those experiences as teachers. The teacher was not saying react out of fear, it was saying let's BE in this moment, let's look at what we are learning from this so we can move forward and not need to experience this lesson again. Simple isn't it? It really is if you live in the moment and ask, what am I learning from this situation? Reacting and basing a choice on fear by creating another limiting rule or creating a program by thinking it will always happen this way, then it always will, and you would have manifested a reoccurring situation in your life. You would have limited your future experiences to always be the hurtful scenario, always validating your core belief, fear.

Fears can be subtle; we think we have worked on all of them, yet there is still a part of our life that is based on fear. If you had a bad break up at one point in your life in a relationship, and now that it is over, you are sure you have worked on that fear and moved beyond it. Then some time later in life you meet someone and it gets serious, and fear pops up to remind us what happened before. Or there is an incident that feels somewhat like something that has happened before, and even though it is not the same thing, the similarity hits a reminder button in the subconscious and boom, fear comes out once again to talk to you.

Fear can affect us in a way where it makes us be too careful in life and keep ourselves from new and wonderful experiences, all based on the fear something will go wrong.

Fear triggers these things inside of us:

> F = Failure becomes an option in our lives.
> E = Ego starts to talk to us loudly.
> A= Activates reaction in us instead of taking action.
> R= Removes us from our inner knowing that we can live in joy and healthy happiness.

As you can see fear can mask itself and make us think it is actually a different emotion. It can present itself as feeling down and that we are a failure, so we will see it as sadness. Sadness is more the secondary emotion, fear is at the root of failure, the issue at hand, and that makes us feel sad. Anger is also a cover up for pain; we get angry instead of feeling hurt inside. Yet again fear is at the core of the hurt, we fear the hurt or of being hurt. Get the idea?

Whatever we are manifesting in our lives is based on what we own inside. So, you can say mentally you have no fear of being hurt or deceived, yet if you do not own it inside, then you will find you are still experiencing things of hurt and deception.

Take your experiences in your life NOW

This will be a meter of what you truly own inside, and it will also tell you what programs you have not worked through yet or are still working on. We work through our programs in layers; they do not vanish over night.

It is important HOW we process them that determine whether we are stuck or are truly moving forward with them. If you linger in the pain and the past then you will be stuck in it, so view it from a different and fresh perspective. Instead of looking at the past events from the same point of view you had when you were living them, look at them from a new you. Look at the events once again as teachers, opportunities for lessons and insights of truth. See them for what they are, scenarios happening to teach us something about others and ourselves.

An example: There was a time in my life I believed I had to fight for all I had and believed in. I grew up in a family full of lies and deception and I was in survival growing up. As an adult, I decided I wanted a different life and truly believed I could have one, and through many layers of it, I have manifested a happy life now. With all of my lessons, I have a choice in how I perceive them. I could look sadly at my early life and carry pain all my life of being unloved, deceived, and hurt, or I can perceive all that it truly was. I was raised by people who were in emotional pain and held onto it, they knew no other way in their life and passed that information to their kids. I could have perceived that things never change and won't get better, and then it wouldn't have. I now perceive my past as great gifts and opportunities. It has helped me to understand true love better; it has assisted me in being very grateful for honesty, for calm, and for being loved. All of my experiences I am more grateful for, because I have experienced both sides of the scales, and without it, I would not have as much wisdom or gratefulness.

It does not mean that you do not acknowledge your sadness or hurt, it means do not become stuck there. Experience it by feeling it, then ask why you feel this way and now that you know why, what can you do to change this so you do not carry this feeling throughout your journey in life.

Tools to Change Perception

Choices I have made in my life, which bring me to what I am experiencing now in my life!

Make a list of what you are experiencing in your life now, joyful or less joyful then go back and look at this list, and ask yourself where is it you made a choice that has led to this event in your now. Then look at what other choice you could have made that would have changed this course of action.

Example: Even if you had gut feelings that a relationship was not the best to encounter, yet you chose to be in the relationship in hopes they would change or you could make it better.

Experience: Now the relationship has gone to a more difficult level and more has happened than you anticipated.

Choice you could have made: Listened to your gut and waited longer to find out more information about this person before deciding to have a relationship.

Different course of action: If you had waited, you would have seen more signs and not engaged in the relationship and waited for what you truly deserved.

Experience	Choice You Could Have Made	Different Course of Action

Let us look at our healthy self and our unhealthy self. Our unhealthy self is part of the ego voice who tells us how unworthy or unlovable we are. The inner voice of the healthy self tell us how lovable and wonderful we are and of our highest potentials. It is amazing that when we see or hear someone say hurtful things to a friend or co-worker, we feel it is unjustified and just plain mean. Our hearts and our bodies react to that behavior. Yet when it comes to our ego voice doing it to our own self, we justify its behavior instead of seeing it as an injustice. When our unhealthy self is speaking to us, we are violating ourselves and this just keeps us small and victimized. Sad but true, we are victimized by our own self. We will react on the unhealthy voice yet rarely act on the healthy voice.

What unhealthy behavior do you inflict on your own self?
Overeating
Not exercising or being active for health
Eating very harmful food for your body and over indulging.
Paying more attention to what you see as your flaws and not your talents.
Seeing more that is wrong with your body than our beauty.
Staying so busy you don't feel joy or hear your inner voice.
Not taking time for rest or fun activities.
Staying in unhealthy relationships.
Not saving money for what you want.
Holding back your feelings from others.
Downplaying a compliment.

Write down all the ones you can think of and add to the list as more come to your attention. Once we put our attention on wanting to know them, we can set our intention to change them, and choose to change them.

Now write a list of all the healthy behaviors you have.
Taking time to rest and have fun and play with friends.
Taking time out to hear your body.
Eating what makes your body feel good and feel healthy.
Exercising.
Saving money for things you want.
Sharing your true feeling with others.
Only engaging in healthy supportive relationships.
Doing stress release activities for your body and emotional being.
Spending time listening and supporting your inner voice.

Now see which list is larger. Only you can CHOOSE to stop the self-abuse!

From this day forward when a fear presents itself to you, write it down and play it out in your head. Write a story telling you the worst that you can imagine that could manifest from this fear. Then go back and read it and ask your inner voice, what would you have learned from the worst that could happen place? Now list these things of what you could learn and choose to learn them now by understanding and embracing them. This way, you fizzle the fear out, because you no longer need to run the fear as the teacher. You know what the lessons are and you choose to learn them more joyfully. Less joyful path, more joyful path, it is always a choice on some level.

Write down the choices you have already made in your life that have brought you to where you are today. Write in all the areas of your life where it fits such as relationship, work, home/family, and friends.

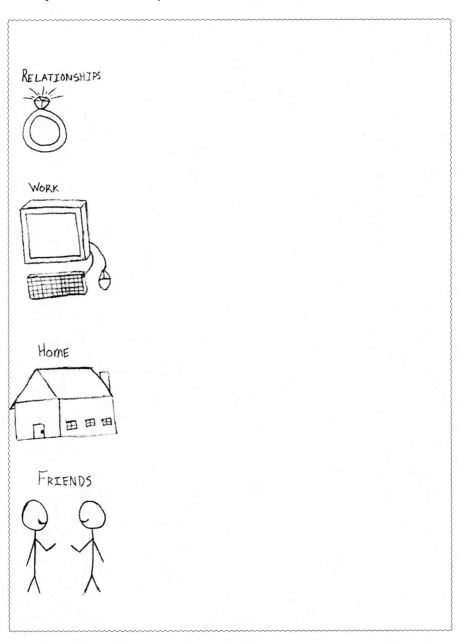

As we grow, it is like metamorphosis, like going from a caterpillar to a butterfly. Make a list of new choices you think would create all new experiences in your life.

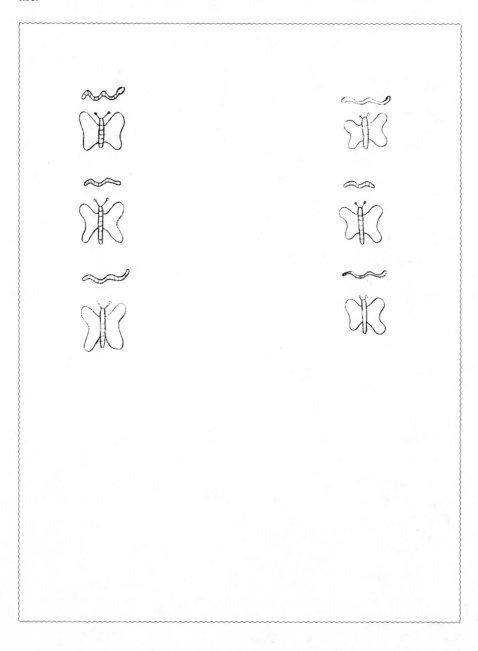

Part II

Presence of Mind

Presence of mind will teach you how to be in your present moment and train yourself not only to listen to your inner voice but to trust yourself as well. This section offers tools to use for transitioning on your journey to your true heart. It will spark your intuition, reminding you that you have had it all along and if you have already acknowledged it, the tools will help you to strengthen your connection. We will explore meditation and exercises that will assist you in both healing and realizing the new life you desire.

Using these tools will help you to move your life into and through the transition.

Keys to Our Intuition

- Sense of Being, It Tells Us About Energy
- Intuition is as Important as All Your Senses
- How to Exercise and Develop Your Intuition
- Listen, Pay Close Attention, and Trust Your Intuition

Our Intuition

Intuition is a sense we have just as we see, hear, smell, and feel. We were all born with it. If we were taught from birth on to listen to our intuition and taught how to cultivate it, it would be as strong as our eyes, ears and sense of touch. We have been trained most of our lives not to pay attention to it and when we enter our school days it is almost unacceptable, yet it is a part of us and it creeps out and visits time and again even if we have worked at ignoring it. Intuition is a part of our senses that tells us about energy.

Do you remember as a young child, when you had no judgments about people? All people are just people, and if we are not shy and we interact with many, we think they are all the same, friendly and sweet. However, maybe there were times when a person came up to say hi, or how cute you were, and you just frowned as a little tike, and did not want them in your space. You did not know why you just did not want to be near them. This was your intuition telling you there was something about that person you did not like. It does not mean they were dangerous but it just could have been they were very negative and you did not want that in your field. Many parents have taught their kids that this way of thinking was not nice. This is one of the ways we were taught not to listen to that feeling. When we are told, say hello to the lady or let that person hug you and don't be mean even though we are having an unpleasant feeling we associate those labels that listening to our intuition was being mean, not to listen to it was being nice etc. I really love watching my grand kids grow up, because my children are allowing them to be their true selves and not forcing them to actions that are against their intuition. Being able to see a generation of young beings grow and stay who they really are inside is exciting and full of wonderful lessons for us adults, to say the least. It calls us to our own issues and calls us to live our truths. I believe this generation that is growing up from the get go to be empowered are all very wise souls teaching us adults.

Let us remember the point where, we had these feelings and look at how they sneak out and still talk with us every once in awhile. Once we remember what it felt like and we realize we always had it and acknowledge this, it will awaken much more within us and begin to be a daily part of our lives again.

So let us start all the way back to, we are all part of God/Source. Every one of us has the living light/breath of God/Source in us, and as we live our lives, we express that life/Source within us out to the world. For now, let us just call it life force energy. Being it is energy, and it has movement, then lets look at how we have been feeling or sensing this life force already in our lives and probably don't even know we are.

Have you ever been in the grocery store and while standing in line, all of the sudden you FEEL something? You do not label it but you know you feel it at your back or on the side of your face. You look and oddly enough, you look in exactly the place where the look is coming from. You turn your head to where your feeling is coming from and you lock eyes with someone who was staring at you. This is because when they focused on you they were sending life force energy to you and your senses of life force energy felt it and responded.

A great example of intuition is mommy's intuition. A mom senses when her children need something, or to check on them, or when they are in a crisis. Our intuition is always on whether we know it or not. We notice it more when it is something BIG that grabs our attention but in reality it is always working. The key to exercising it and making it stronger is to be conscious of it, even the subtle times it is at work, such as you think of someone and then they call you soon after. The more we are conscious of our intuition and acknowledge it the more we are aware of it and count on it.

You may wonder why you do not always feel this then. Most people do when they are not over busy in their mind. Although, someone who has exercised it and developed it probably does feel it most times. When you have not developed it, it comes in moments of quietness in the mind. This is why meditation is so good, it not only relaxes us, but it assists us in hearing our inner life force, our higher voice within. We think and feel more clearly and we do this because we are using ALL of our senses.

Our intuition is important as it assists and guides us to what we do not realize in our left-brain. Have you ever driven down the road and all of the sudden you wanted to take a different way to work; to find out later, you avoided an accident? This is your intuition, your inner voice talking to you. The more you pay attention to it or learn to listen to it, the more it will assist you in clear choices and direction in life. How great would that be? Many people are afraid of their intuition or they think it is outside our selves and is maybe bad or negative. I have to ask then, why would every person on the planet have had an encounter with his or her inner voice, if it were not meant that we all have it as a natural sense? You will have to decide what you feel on your own. If you ask, and you hear an answer, it is your inner voice that is talking to you.

To get back in touch with your intuition it sometimes takes practice. When we numb something out or turn it off it is like a muscle that got flabby from no exercise or attention put on it. We have to tone it up and get it back in shape so to speak. Start paying attention to when you are out and about in the world. Do you pass someone in the store and get a feeling, whether emotional or a feeling somewhere in your body? Pay attention to how many times this happens: you are driving down the road and you are in your lane passing by others in their lane next to you, all of the sudden you slow down, and look over at a car and just do not feel comfortable. The next thing you know they are switching into your lane and not paying attention to where they are going. These things are always happening in your life. What tones and exercises your intuition is to be conscious that these things are happening and to acknowledge them. Your intuition is the same thing as your inner voice, just different labels. Our inner voice always talks to us, but after spending much time in life ignoring it, we think we do not have it like others. If you told someone great information every day that would assist them and they ignored you every day, wouldn't you stop telling them? However, if they started paying attention, or asked for your information, you would tell them again. The inner voice is the same way. If you ask to hear the inner voice again and be conscious of it talking to you, it will start again. The more you act on the information, the more you will get. Even if you are one of the people who numbed yourself to hearing your inner voice, you still have felt it or had it talk to you; you just did not acknowledge it. Have you ever walked in a room to just feel UCK, and was not sure why? It could have been someone in a bad mood or distressed in the room. We usually just chalk it up, as huh, weird, wonder why I felt like that and then we let it go. Most times when I work with clients who have left bad relationships or are leaving one, we always conclude on some level they had a bad gut feeling before they got into it, but because they did not know why or have any proof of what they were feeling, they disregarded it. So, we have never numbed out the feeling or the inner voice itself, we just stopped being conscious of it and acting on it. We need to learn once again to pay attention to it and to trust it.

Many people when they are trying to learn or be aware of listening to their inner guidance are very hung up on where the guidance is coming from. They ask me, is it my guide, my angel, my soul, or is it from God? Everyone is going to label it something different according to his or her own belief system. There really is no right or wrong answer. What I do know is that you get a feeling in your gut when you know it is information for you. Many times, it is a very good and warm feeling in your heart, and other times it is a knowing, you just know it! In all of these cases, your inner being is saying it is correct information for you. So I would not be caught up on whom or where it is coming from. If you must label it, just go in and ask.

The most important thing NOT to do is try to interpret what you receive, but instead learn the right questions to ask. If you get a feeling or message not to engage in a deal, you can ask, is this not for my higher good and the highest good of others? Or you can just learn to trust that if it feels not good or like a big no, then go with it. One thing I always say is that my inner voice is spirit, just to label it for me, and one thing I know, if we are listening and paying attention, then when spirit says move, you just got to move. If it is a very big decision in life, I always have felt the feeling very strong, so I feel compelled to act on it. It is not hard to listen or be aware of your higher guidance. If you are consciously asking to be in tune with it then you will be. It is trusting and acting on it that seems to be the one aspect people have to learn to do.

Another great way to understand this is to watch children out in the world, young kids two to five years old. They display using their intuition all the time and you can learn from them by watching them.

> Intuition is feeling or knowing energy, life force and it is guiding you or tell-
> ing you where other life force energy is coming from, such as the stare in the
> grocery store. Once you understand this about energy you can then understand
> even better why and how The Law of Attraction works as one of the universal
> laws.

List on the next page times you remember using your intuition. Notice the feeling you get inside as you list them. It could be as simple and childlike as when you just get a feeling to stop at a store you were not originally going to stop at. On arriving, you run into a friend and have a happy chat but are glad you ran into each other. When we were very young, we just acted on our feelings inside and the promptings of our inner voice. This is because we knew it was a natural part of ourselves and not something outside of ourselves.

List events that you remember in your life where you have used your intuition

Keys to Meditation

- Helps to Relieve Stress from the Body and Mind
- Helps to Quiet Mind and Ego so we Can Hear Our Inner Voice
- Any Meditation is better than none at All
- Inner Voice and Acknowledging Ego
- Examples of Meditations
- Meditations to Work through the Layers

Meditation

Meditation is very important! It is beneficial for a healthy mind and body because it relieves stress from the body and the mind. The more relaxed and calm our bodies are, the healthier they will be. The more calm our mind and emotions are the healthier our emotional selves are. It is also an important tool to use to get in touch with our inner voice. The inner voice is our Higher self, or soul self and is wise. Now, your higher self/inner voice is different from your intuition. Your intuition is kind of like an aspect of the higher self. It works more on a feeling, maybe a warning when for example you are walking somewhere that could be dangerous. Your wise soul/higher self knows this, and gives you a signal through your intuition. Many times I get a gut feeling and have no idea why, yet I have learned from many times of validation, it is always a good thing to listen. Now, if I get a feeling, and I trust my intuition, I then can ask my higher self why and I will get information that is more detailed. The Higher self is different, and is talking more to your own higher being.

Meditation helps you quiet your mind and ego so that you can hear your inner voice. After you get used to hearing your inner voice you do not always have to be in a meditative state to hear it, but it still helps when wanting more detailed and clear information. As I mentioned before there are many levels of meditation, but I am not going to cover deeper states of meditation in this book. We all have to start somewhere and this is a good place to start when first learning about it.

Many will say that you have to be in a deeper state of meditation to hear your higher self; I do not personally believe this to be true and I know from my experiences with my students that it is not true for them. There are also schools of thought that teach that you have to be in a lotus position or some other physically uncomfortable position to meditate, again not true. If those types of meditations are good for you then by all means do them, I am just pointing out they are not the only types of meditation and the one's I suggest here also work to a certain level. Start with simple steps and then explore other forms of meditations.

When most people first start training their self to hear their inner voice, they will doubt it. The common theme I hear is it feels too much like me. Well there is a good reason for that, IT IS YOU! It is important to learn that your higher self/soul is not separate from you and is not outside of yourself. I give this example to my clients or when I teach children about their soul. Take your hand and put it in a glove, and then wiggle your fingers around, your hand is animating the glove. So, think of your soul, as slipping inside a large glove we call our body and animating it. It is very much YOU, so of course your inner voice will feel and sound like you. It is true though; that in the beginning you can have a difficult time knowing the difference between higher self and ego, but this is why meditation is so important. When we get used to quieting the mind and the ego, we will be able to discern what our ego is and what our higher self is. It just takes practice.

Begin Meditating!

When we first start meditating, it seems as if our mind and ego want to be much louder. This is true but the more you fight it or try to push thoughts away, the more it seems to get louder. I suggest you acknowledge the thought and or feeling and just say thank you and let it go. A good example is as soon as you start to get quiet; your grocery list goes through your head. This is normal, as no one likes to be brushed off or stifled including your own thoughts and mind chatter. Like us, your thoughts want your attention. So go ahead and acknowledge them. You might say, thank you for reminding me of that and I will file it away over here for when I need it. The more you do this to each mind chatter that comes up, it will calm down and know it does not need to be so loud.

Now ego, that is a different story. Ego wants to say things like, hey you, you have dishes to do, kids to watch, and you do not have time for this. Another is you will never be able to meditate so just give it up now. Ego has always tried to protect us from something, or it has bought into one of our negative patterns telling us it is a truth about us. Ego believes it is helping you by reminding you of the "thing" it perceives as a truth about you. It had a job. However if you continue to allow ego to run the show that job actually becomes self-sabotage. Being told and reminded about a negative pattern, such as, "you will never do well" may cause you to stop trying to be successful in fear that you will fail and be devastated. So, all these years, ego feels it has done its job keeping you safe and in your place. It panics if you try to tell it to shut up.

Many classes back in the day taught to shut ego off or ignore it or push it away. I feel the following exercise has always worked better with most of my clients. I tell my clients to dialogue with their ego. Tell your ego, I thank you for always telling me that, but we have a new mission now, a higher mission, and this is what it is. Now, I need you to remind me of this new mission. You might state that mission as "We now love our self and know we deserve better." Ask ego to always give you an alert message when you think opposite of this. You can actually do a wonderful meditation where you breathe and relax, and then see yourself on a beautiful mountaintop. Invite your ego to join you. You can visualize your ego as a person or some image that you can identify with for ego. Then dialogue with this ego image and show ego your now new and higher vision. Sit down and talk out how ego can assist you to fulfill this higher view and life for yourself. Many times after clients have done this meditation several times, they say the image of ego changes each time it comes to the mountain, which has been an indication of the transformation for them.

You might feel awkward at first when doing these types of visual meditations but like anything unfamiliar to you in life, the more you practice them, the more comfortable and creative you will get.

So many of my clients tell me they cannot meditate. They usually have a pre-conceived idea of what meditation is. So, I ask them, have you ever been washing dishes and then noticed an amount of time passed and you were not aware of it? Or, have you been driving or vacuuming and this has happened? This is a form of going in the meditative state. It is just being there unconsciously. Conscious meditation can be practiced and then with a quiet mind you will be able to hear your inner voice more clearly.

Some people do better by doing a moving meditation, such as walking, Tai Chi, or body movement. Just because you are moving does not mean you are not meditating. It is important to clear our thoughts and to get the mind still and quiet so we can hear our wiser voice. It is relaxing, healthy for the body, and it reduces stress.

Breathing in meditation is very important. Breath is energy, and breath is a great catalyst to focus and use to move things that are stuck in our mind, our emotions, and our physical body. Breath when focused on in cyclic motion can be very relaxing, not to mention also rejuvenating. You may feel as if you had a great nap afterwards.

The next time you have tension in any part of your body, close your eyes, and just start taking very deep breaths. Breathe all the way to the bottom of your toes and then release it slowly. After doing this for four to five breathes, focus on the part of the body that was tense. There is still probably some tension left there. Then focusing on that part of the body, take a deep breath and in your mind see yourself breathing into the part of the body with the tension. Then as you slowly breathe out, see, or feel the tension leave that part of the body. Do this for several breaths and you will see that you have released the tension. If you do this for all areas left in the body that is holding tension, when you have completed you will have released the stress from your physical body. While you were focusing on the tense areas and releasing that tension, at the same time without noticing it, you had relaxed your busy mind. Isn't that great!

There are many forms and many ways to meditate. Every morning this is one of the many I do depending how I feel:

Take deep breaths all the way down to your toes and as you breathe out, let go of all thoughts. With each breath, tell yourself you are bringing in the light of source/God, and breathing out all worries, all negative, all stress and tensions in the body and mind. Once you feel relaxed, say in your mind, you are bringing Source energy down from Source, in your crown, and down through your body, down and out your feet, and into the core of the Mother Earth. Then state you are bringing the energy back up from Mother Earth and back up through your feet, and as it comes back in, see or say it is creating a figure eight (infinity symbol) as it flows back up into Source. Do not make it a color; let it be what color it wants, (may be different on different days). State that this energy will continue to flow throughout the day as a figure eight. Then see bright threads of light in all the colors that they can be and see them come down from Source and wrap you in a beautiful blanket of threads of light. After you are all wrapped in these lights, seal the outer part of this cocoon first in emerald green light and then in turquoise light. See how different your day is!

There are days that I do not have time, but not often, because making time for me and to make myself more relaxed and clear is a choice I make. But, if I got up late to the alarm or for whatever reason, I just did not have my regular morning time then I do this quick meditation:

While I take my shower, I focus on the breathing again, and after several cleansing breaths I focus on the water. My thoughts (energy) focus on being cleansed, and so in my mind I say, "Cleaning away all that is not mine or is not of my highest good today." I intend to bring in all lessons joyfully and ask that I be clear and open to seeing the lessons and learning them. I ask as the water is falling, to bring love into my heart and that all I pass today or talk with today, I learn from them and assist them in whatever they need for their highest good. Please use me as an instrument of love today.

Use your own wording and have fun with it. Think of different ways that work for you, there is no right or wrong with it.

Now there are forms of deeper meditations, but begin with what works for you and if you want to learn others later, you will be guided by your own inner voice to seek them out.

The more you meditate and in longer intervals, the stronger this sense becomes. You will get to a point that anytime you need clarity, you can just take a few deep cleansing breaths, and quiet your mind in a matter of seconds. This is very handy because this is what will assist you in being more in tune and hearing your inner guidance (intuition). This is very helpful in any circumstances in life and especially in moments of confusion where you feel you need clarity or you need to have clear answers to take action.

Anytime we need to make choices in life, it is best to do this from this state, the state of being in touch with your inner guidance. So, each time we need to make a choice in life, take a few deep breaths, and clear the mind chatter and then tune into yourself and ask the question about your choice. How great it will feel for you to always make clear choices in life and make them from your inner guidance, as this makes for more joyful choices and results.

When we make choices in life this way, we are making them from our whole heart, and that heart in a healing space or healed states chooses the more joyful path. With our hearts fully opened, we make our choices from the place of our highest good and from the place of for the good of all involved.

It is a good thing to practice different forms of meditation until you find one that resonates with you. If you do not like the form you choose, you are more likely not to want to continue with it, or think it is not working for you. Meditation is better when you feel the desire to meditate, not forcing yourself to. If you are saying I have to, or I should, then it is not from the heart that you want this, and then it becomes just another task you have to add to your daily list. If you see meditation as a tool for spending sacred time with yourself, to nurture and rejuvenate yourself, then the time you set aside to meditate is really taking time to spend with yourself and love yourself. In this way, it is never a chore.

Meditation as a Tool/Working through Our Layers

Once you become comfortable at meditating and being more relaxed you may want to explore other ways that meditation can work as a tool. First become comfortable with being connected to your inner voice and learning to trust what it tells you. Then branch out and combine meditation and listening to your inner voice to actively work through some of your layers to get to know your true self better.

Start by entering the relaxed state and connecting with your inner voice, then ask your inner voice to show you and assist you to understand what your programs are, which are what you have created your story on. Know that we can change our story and how we want to walk our journey here on earth at any time. It is a choice. Keep a journal for after meditation and by the bed. Many times when we are first working consciously on our self, we have dreams that are significant in giving us pieces to our story we do not remember in the awake state. Journaling is good on all levels. I kept a journal for seventeen years and every New Year's I would write a positive statement of what I wanted to work on and achieve that year coming. I would write my desires and dreams to start the year. Then every Christmas Eve I would re read my entire year journal and it would amaze me how much I had changed and grown. My journal would actively show me how much I had changed my perceptions about how I saw my journey. Many times as we are changing and growing, we do not realize how much of a leap we have taken in growth, so reflecting back through the journals is a nice validation.

You can also use the journal as a workbook for your exercises in your growth. It does not matter what time of year you start your journal or choose to review it, I chose personally for me New Years and Christmas Eve, but feel free to make your own time periods for this.

You may want to try this exercise. Write any programs you know you have and then list at what age you chose those programs and why you chose them. Write as many as you can think of.

Example: I will never sing in public, I am not good at it.

I got it at eight years old when I was in a play at school and I made that assumption and rule because I was teased about how badly I sang.

Program	Age Acquired

Now take each one of these and ask if you really still need any of them. If not, ask inside how or what steps you can take to change this rule and choose a different story.

Steps I will take to change this:

A great tool that assists us in finding programs is to make a list of emotional chords that push our buttons. To help you identify some of these emotional chords, fill in the sentence below.

NEVER refer to me as_____, because it makes me feel _____.

Examples:
Never refer to me as <u>weak</u>, because it makes me feel <u>like a victim</u>.
Never refer to me as my <u>mother</u>, because it makes me feel <u>inadequate</u>.

NEVER refer to me as_____, because it makes me feel _____.
NEVER refer to me as_____, because it makes me feel _____.
NEVER refer to me as_____, because it makes me feel _____.

Writing these sentences assists us in bringing up old programs that we carry inside whether we are conscious of them or not. If we feel them as an emotional reaction inside then they are still very alive inside of us. This will help to tell you what is still stuck in your subconscious.

Pay attention to your physical body, your thoughts, and your feelings when you read and answer each sentence. Any emotional reaction, any part of the physical body that tenses or feels nauseated, or any disturbing thoughts or memories that may surface are what I am calling a chord. If it charges (causes a reaction) us in any way such as your mind, body, or emotional reaction, then it is attached to an event that has created a memory and a block within us. Pay attention to your body, it is talking to you. Once you have identified these chords, which act as blocks in our life, then you will want to choose one or two of these at a time to start actively working on to release and heal from your life.

Exercise: Healing journey

One way to work on these old programs is to use the techniques below. First let us take the sentences you just answered, and let us take the example of never refer to me as weak; it makes me feel like a victim. In one of the techniques below I will write the scenario as if this is the issue you are working on. When you take the guided healing journey, insert your own words and symbols.

Take a few deep breaths and get quiet and calm inside. When your mind chatter is off start to visualize yourself lying somewhere that is your favorite place, it could be a meadow, forest or a comfy bed. After you are comfortable, ask your inner voice to show you where you first got this program of being told you were weak or a victim. A person or a time period may present itself or a symbol representing where this program came from. See chords of light coming from the image that has appeared or that you sense and see this chord connected to you from the person or image. Pay attention where the chord is attached to you. Is it your solar plexus, heart, or head area? Ask your higher self, angelic helpers or God/Goddess to assist you in understanding why you took this program on and what you learned from it. When you feel you have clarity ask your higher self or helpers to cut all chords that are attached to this situation and as they are being cut, forgive them and yourself and understand that these were just lessons in your life. Ask that anything else connected to this situation that is not of your higher learning and higher good be released and healed. See the chords release themselves from you. Then ask to call back to you all of your life force energy and to transform that energy into the highest light. Here, ask that you call to yourself strength and empowerment and know you are a capable soul to handle all of your lessons in life. Ask to learn and be clear of your lessons daily and to draw to you situations that are filled with love and of your highest learning and highest good. Gently come out of the healing journey and take some time to write your experience in a journal.

You can use this meditation as a tool to assist you with any of the chords that surfaced that you seem to be having difficulty disconnecting from and healing.

Take a few deep breaths and get quiet and calm inside, when mind chatter is off, visualize your issue or a symbol to represent that issue. Then ask your higher self, angels etc … to show you what the wall around this issue looks like. Be open to what you see. Some will see a wall like a Ft. Knox; some have seen wooden walls, rock walls. The symbology will let you know how much of a block this particular issue is. After you see the wall clearly, ask for help and guidance to work through this wall. You may take one brick at a time out. You may blow the wall up or dissolve it. When you feel the wall is down or dissolved, ask for assistance to understand the lesson and to heal the place where the wall once was. When you feel at peace with the healing gently come out of it. Write the experience in your journal.

It may take many meditations to take the wall down slowly, only do what is comfortable. You may not feel at the moment it is doing anything, but it IS! If you keep taking the wall down, you will start to notice progress with this issue in your waking time life. Do it and see.

Other Reasons and Ways of Using Meditation

We do not always have to have a question, program, or issue to work on in meditation. It is a tool we can use to be still inside and deepen our connection with our Self and our heart. It is a tool to relax, rejuvenate or to focus on what we want in our lives. Meditation is a good place to see and feel what our life's dreams are and find and explore our passions. We can listen to music or a CD of nature sounds and just ride them and see where our meditation takes us.

Chants might be something that you prefer to do also. Explore all different forms of meditation until you find what feels right for you. It does not have to be just one technique either. Why not find many you like and do them according to how you feel that particular day? Another that is a favorite of mine is to chant the HU, for me it is a way I start my meditations. Now when I HU for several minutes I am immediately centered and feel very calm and open inside. Then I just allow the meditation to unfold. There are many tones such as HU and OM or AUM that people choose to chant. Again, you should find what feels right for you and research what the tones vibration represents. Be conscious of your choice. Here is information of HU only because this is the one I most frequently choose for myself.

Sit in a comfortable position and take a few deep breaths until you feel relaxed and your mind is clear. Hold your attention on the space that would be the center of your head, a place called Kether. (It is ok if you do not know exactly where this is, just start by focusing between your eyes.) Take a deep breath in and as you release that breath sing the tone HU (sounds like Hugh). Start with ten minutes a day and you can work your way up to twenty minutes. As you do this allow the experience to unfold. You may have an intent when you do this of wanting clarity or talking with guides or masters on your journey in life for insight and teachings. (Many believe the HU is an old Tibetan chant and that the tone is the vibration of Soul). You will have to seek your clarity on this for yourself. It may take time for you to feel an open link, but if you continue to do this, you will gain great clarity with the intent of wanting clarity in your life.

Another favorite of mine is to meditate in nature. It assists me in feeling the connection to the planet and my environment. I open my heart and feel myself emanating love to the world and all life forms and I am open to receiving the love back from the planet. There is a lot of love on this planet and with all the fear based news and media out there, we tend to forget how much love and joy there really is that exists. One way to remember and actually experience it is to meditate and open your self to tune into it and receive. It is a wonderful reminder of how much good, love and joy is on the planet.

The picture below is where I drew the large box as my inner voice and then the little radio broadcasting to me was my ego, hidden and subtle. Now draw an image on a piece of paper of your inner voice and then your ego voice, be creative, and have fun.

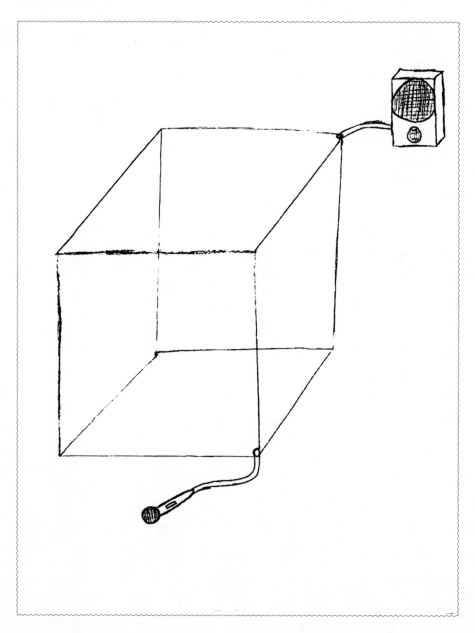

Part III

Moving Forward

We have explored some areas in our lives in the first part of this book that may be holding us back. There are tools and reflections there to assist us in releasing and healing our past. Healing our past and inner self is the beginning of the journey to discovering self and to become more aware of what is happening in our lives. We have looked through layers of who we were, molded by life's experiences, and uncovered our true self within those false layers. We have explored and utilized tools to assist us in healing within.

Now it is time to add some concepts and healing ways to walk forward as your new and authentic true heart. The pages to follow are about manifesting what we truly want in life, to live and walk our journeys more awakened, and to have more heightened and richer experiences in life. It is time to move forward knowing you are now creating consciously every moment to come. You have created your reality in life all along, but now it will be through the eyes of awareness, knowing in each moment on a conscious level you're choosing your steps from here on out. It is about staying aware of the lessons in the moment, now that the past has been released and healed. Every moment is a new experience and a new adventure that you are manifesting the new self, which is who you always were all along anyway, before you forgot.

So get ready to find out how to walk this journey manifesting your dreams!

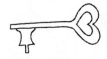

Keys to the Power in Words

- Words Create and Change Our Perceptions
- Words Are Powerful and Assist to Empower
- Words Are Just As Powerful if Not More Then Action
- Choose the Words That Are More Correct to What You Want to Manifest
- Words Are Reflecting What Our True Desire Is

The Power in Words

Words are very powerful and assist us in changing our perception of things in life. You may not believe in the words you are using at first but if you use new and more positive words with power, eventually your subconscious will agree to them.

Most times when people are communicating, they do it unconsciously, not really paying attention to what they are really saying, and many times end up saying things they are not intending to. Living from our heart and soul means to truly be conscious of every waking moment, every choice we make and what we are communicating out to the world. Be AWARE! In doing so, we are being accountable and paying attention in the now, in the moment of what we are manifesting around us.

Let me give you an example of how we might be saying things we do not really mean to intend. I saw this man in the grocery store with his daughter who was about eight years old. A woman walked up to them and said hello, I have not seen you in a long time. The man said hello and then said to his daughter, you remember Miss Brag, she was your kindergarten teacher. The little girl said no, she did not remember. The man grabbed the girl's arm, with a little squeeze, and said of course you do sweetie, this is Miss Brag; you remember (with force in his voice) she was your teacher and you really like her. Well, she did not remember and after Miss Brag walked away, he jerked the little girl's arm and said, when I tell you yes you remember, just say you do, ok? Now you embarrassed me.

Well, I am sure he was thinking more of his discomfort, but what he just REALLY told his daughter, was next time just lie. I am sure this is not what was in his mind at the time, and I am sure he would have never just said, "Hey lie next time," but in the way he communicated to her he indeed just told her that. It is important that we are conscious of what we say, and what we truly mean, otherwise we give mixed messages out to the universe and in doing so call back to us mixed experiences. Not all of what we actually intended.

This is just one of many areas we want to look at on our soul journey in dealing with the power of words. Stop, think, and communicate what it is you TRULY mean. Be clear first on what it is you truly mean. The man could have seen his daughter was acting out of truth and innocence, she really did not remember, and it was his issue that her not remembering had embarrassed him. We do not honor anyone by lying even when we think it is saving him or her from hurt feelings. Honoring someone is to be honest with him or her and it is honoring yourself.

Choosing Your Words

In order to understand what we truly mean, we need to re-evaluate how we choose our words now, or do we even choose them? Are they just coming out of our mouth automatically? We need to look at how we communicate now, and maybe if our words are automatic, it is more what we mean inside than we are aware of. It is like when we say, we are abundant, we are always provided for, and we are working on knowing that inside of us. Then when in a casual conversation such as talking with a friend at lunch, you might say without thinking, I am so broke, and looking at my next few months, I have no place that I can see relief coming to me. Well, what just happened here is your true belief of what is happening and will happen just came out of your mouth. You just said you were broke, yet if you were asking for abundance in life, you need to see where you are already abundant and not look at the areas in your life as lack.

Then you proceed home and read your positive words one more time that are taped to your bathroom mirror, on "I am abundant" and "I am provided for." You may be saying these words, but what you said to your friend really is reflecting what you still believe in your subconscious and fear has spoken through you. Many of you may wonder why your affirmations are not working despite saying them everyday and having them posted around your house. The problem is that the universe responds to the emotional energy of what is inside of you. Affirmations may be a tool to help bring to the forefront of your consciousness what you want your inner reality to be however if you truly feel lack and fear and an absence of abundance as reflected in your words this is what the universe will reflect back to you.

You may be wondering, but if I really did not have the money, then what would I have said? One way to change the energy here is saying to your friend, I was abundant enough to pay all my bills, and after choosing to pay them, I am manifesting more abundance now to have other things in my life as well.

It is not enough to just say more positive words and not work on it inside to own those words. You can replace words that are disempowering for words that are positive empowering words as this helps to reprogram or deprogram the subconscious. However, this alone will not convince you, it still takes conscious work to truly own those words. If you pay attention to what words you use more often in your life, it can act as a tool of where your subconscious beliefs still are and provide you with a place to start working with.

Take a small spiral notebook with you in your pocket or purse and every time you use disempowering words write them down. Then when you use them again put a little check mark next to them to see how many times you use this word or phrase. As many times as you use it, is as many times you enforce this thought and belief and in doing this, what you are manifesting in your life. Let us look at some more frequently used words.

Can't
There is no such thing. You can do anything. In reality, you are saying you won't or that you choose not to.
Try
Failure is inherent in this word.
If
If is very common. It calls up an endless cycle of fears.

IF is a never-ending cycle of possible outcomes based on fears of moving forward whether in thought or by action.
You can say IF to everything and it leads to a million probabilities. Yes, there are roads of probability, but we choose which one we want to step onto, and when we use the word IF, we are saying the road or experience is choosing us and we have no choice in the matter. The word "IF" will get you chasing your tail every time especially when brought into a cross road you have encountered in life or into any meditations.

Let us just take these for now and write them as you say or think them, then put a check mark next to how many times you use them. In my classes, I use muscle testing with my students on these words, and when you test the body, it shows a decrease in energy and this is because they are disempowering words. When you use the opposite, it supports the body, mind, and spirit and is a definite, which means you own what you are saying. Therefore, if you are using these words often, think of how much you are disempowering yourself or how much energy is being leaked away.

Do this exercise for a week. Then for the second week work on taking them out of your vocabulary all together. You may want to start with just one or two at a time, so you can truly master this. Even if you slip and say try, then immediately change it to will or choose to.

Here are some ideas for alternative words to use:
Replace try with will or choose to.
Replace can't with I will, I choose to, I desire to.
Replace if or what if with This—will occur, the outcome will be of the highest good, this path will lead me here _____.

After you have done this, and it may take awhile until you have truly taken these phrases out of your vocabulary, see what difference it has made in your life and journal this.

These are just the words most commonly used and the ones that subtly sabotage your path of manifesting. There are other words or phrases we use unconsciously that also sabotage our growing and our learning. One of these words is should. Whenever we say we should do something or should be a certain way, we are saying it does not come from love, from our hearts. We are saying based on someone else's thoughts or judgments we think we should. This is never making the choice from the heart and the place of love. Should is usually an indication there are behind the scene feelings of fears of being judged or feeling guilt. If we do an action from "should" we are reacting from fear or guilt and in doing so, it is a self-based ego choice. It is not about the other person, it is actually that we do not want to feel guilt or we do not want someone to judge us, so it is an act of selfishness not selflessness. Not only do we want to be aware of the words we use daily, but in truth why we are using them. This is where keeping a journal on them can assist you in seeing issues you still need to work on. In this case, it would be working on not feeling guilt and not fearing judgment.

Conscious Clarity

Another reason we want to be conscious of the words we use is to be clear on why we are at the place we are in our life, how we are manifesting experiences and the way we perceive them? When we are being conscious of what words we choose and choosing them to truly reflect what we are calling in, we are manifesting with conscious clarity. Many have the right frame of mind when first opening to their conscious path. They have all the sincerity of getting answers, but they do not have the words for asking clearly what they want and then wonder why they are constantly working on one specific thing for a lengthy time. Many people will continually say I want to release _____; this could be victim, survival and so forth. Well, you can release it in the moment, but then you will experience it again when you do not work on the reason why you own victim or survival. Look at the question this way; please make clear to me why I am validating a victim or survival mode and assist me in seeing and learning the lesson in order to release this pattern and live healthy.

I have had students that ask me to make them more spiritual, or to bring back to them the time when they could feel and know their guides were there, and assist them in finding their intuition. None of these things went anywhere, so let us word them this way. Assist me in knowing my own block to my spirituality and assist me in being open once again to this aspect of myself. Assist me in knowing my block to seeing and feeling my guides and to know how to move this block and heal it within me. Assist me in knowing clearly, what my block is to my intuition and to know how to work through it and heal this inside of me.

Or when people say let me get the answer in the dreamtime, more specifically could say to assist me to get the answer in the dreamtime and remember the dream, and be clear of its meaning. Otherwise, you can know you had the dream but not remember it, or you dream and remember it and have no clue what it means.

It is about getting in touch with the place inside you that you truly want to express and know how to express what your true heart wants.

One of my favorite examples of the power of words comes from when I teach. This is more common than you think. I will take the group on a guided meditation, and they will have a clear and profound experience. Then when they are in the waking moment to write it all down and then share with the class, they will say, I think I got this, or I think I might have seen this. Either you did or you did not. When I say that, they say well, it could have been wrong, or I was making it up. Again not saying what they truly meant the first time, they KNEW they saw it, but they were afraid of judgment from class members so I THINK sounded better, as in not sure in case I was wrong. It is more empowering to just say, I saw this clearly, but I have fears that it is my mind making stuff up, how do I work through that? This person's lesson is still to learn trust in self and self worth. This is why they think and not know yet. When we trust our self and become confident then comes certainty.

Repeated Lessons

A message or a lesson will visit us many times in layers as we talked about early in the book. We repeat things until we get it. The universe whispers, then talks loudly, and then yells until we hear it. These lessons also visit us in layers, because we get it in a process, so it is also bringing us to these places within us.

> I think I got it.
> I know I got it.
> I am certain I got it.

What happens once we are certain we are done visiting that lesson? When we are certain that we own it inside ourselves, it is one with us, and there is no more doubt to it we then manifest that what we truly want in our life. We do not have to keep visiting the lesson by experiencing less joyful situations.

When we manifest in our lives we also want to be sure we are not only using power words but also that we are saying clearly what we want. Many times, we think we are saying it very clear and yet when it comes in a different way than what we think we asked for, we are confused why this has happened. No matter how long we practice this until we live it; we still have those times where we learn from trial and error. The lesson we still need to learn always presents itself though.

Here is a good example. I had been living my life a long time with the consciousness of manifesting and being clear on what I ask for, yet this event was another lesson in life, of don't presume the universe will bring it the way you think. I was almost done with this book and some financial issues came up, which I was not surprised, because I walk through my lessons before I share them, so I figured there was another layer of trust to be learned here. I clearly stated (I thought) what my intention was. I stated I would like ten thousand dollars so I can finish my book stress free and I will be able to focus on the creative side and finish the book by December 12.

Now my thoughts were the ten thousand would allow all my debts paid and I could focus just on finishing the book and not having to take great amounts of work in and work overtime. A woman I work with and am friends with owns an Inn, and with those properties, she owns two beautiful cliff side ocean properties, with a great view, privacy, sounds of the ocean, and a hot tub. She knew I was not done with my book and so she gifted my son, the wolf and I both houses for two and a half weeks that the Inn would be shut down for the season. I took the gift with great gratitude and trusted it would all be ok. Well, the place was definitely stress free, I did in fact finish the book, and until one night my son decided for the heck of it to add up what both houses would have been for that time period, I had no idea it was ten thousand dollars. HELLO ANNE, HELLO UNIVERSE! I had to laugh, for it was exactly what I asked for, stress free, ten thousand dollars, and finish the book. After I laughed on how I once again forgot to add in there, ten thousand dollars in my bank account. I thanked the universe and added, and now can you assist me in manifesting the money I need to pay all the bills and then some for this month and do it while I am here at the beach house that does not interfere with me writing the book. This happened also while I was there.

So, many times when we feel we are being clear in our words, we are not. I always see the lessons in everything so I did see where this was a great lesson in two areas. One, I manifested damn well, and two, no matter how long you have been walking this journey and walking the talk, you are still human and in a body and have to be reminded of the laws once again ~ Be Clear!

Make a list of words you feel are powerful and pay attention to ones you say that feel draining. Close your eyes, take a few deep breaths and say a word, you will feel a sinking feeling in your gut if it is not a power word, and you will feel strength or excited feeling when it is a powerful word. Divide a piece of paper in half and write the less powerful words on one side, then write the opposite of that word on the right side. Write the ones on the right on a small notebook and carry them around to remind you to choose powerful words.

Another great tool is to take a word you want to own inside and feel you do not own yet, such as power. Then do the following walking exercise everyday for ten minutes until you feel it and reach the last stage of the exercise. Walk ten minutes first two days saying. "I walk into my power" saying it repeatedly with every step, and remember to breathe. When it feels strong and like you own it, then start walking it the next few days saying "I walk in my power" then when this feels strong, do it for two days saying, "I am power" You can do this with any word you want to own as embodiment of the energy. Use abundance, open heart, love, healing, anything at all, add your own words.

> First two days: I walk into my _____.
> When it feels strong and you own it
> Next few days: I walk in my _____. When this feels strong
> Two more days: I am _____.

You might ask why this walking meditation? An action assists the subconscious to break a program much faster or to accept a new one. Walking is a good action or writing. Many people process in their head but you will find that once you put it to paper, it seems to shift, change, and begin to move much quicker.

Write power words in the universal screen that you are broadcasting out now!

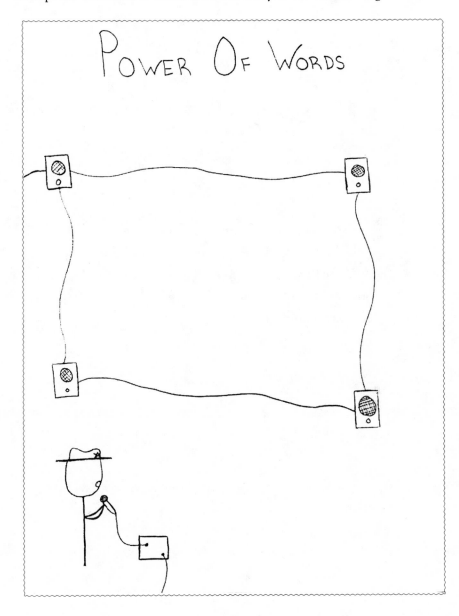

Keys to Universal Laws

- We Are Making Changes at an Accelerated Rate
- Universal Laws, Not a Secret
- How These Laws Apply in Your Life
- Affirmations vs. Intentions
- Create Intent for the Day

Universal Laws

Things to Know On the Journey

It always starts with needing to heal our past, recognize our programs and our trigger chords. We need to be able to understand how we became who we are and how to get to being our true heart self. It used to be a long time ago in seminars and awareness classes, that we would spend years just on healing the inner child, then moving up to learning that we actually create our own life and experiences and even in that teaching it was slowly introduced in layers. In the time we are in now, as I mentioned in the beginning of the book, we are in a 5D time and an accelerated time. It has been shown and I have experienced in my coaching work, that it is most helpful to learn more about the universal laws in the beginning of a person's journey to self-healing. In these accelerated times of change, people are more open and look more and more into alternative help. I want to stop here for a moment and point out many of these teachings were never alternative and actually existed long before our modern way of psychology and self-help workshops began. I am not saying they are not good and useful tools, I am just saying they were more the new way. These other teachings are ancient and existed long before we had psychology on the planet and are not actually alternative. In all cases, I believe that both worlds are complimentary, the word alternative suggests they are separate and an either or choice when in reality, what we call now as traditional ways are actually NOT traditional. Natural awareness and inner healing was traditional. Again, I am not suggesting one is better than the other or that we should not explore both, what I am suggesting is that both have strong and healthy points and are complimentary to each other.

Back to how accelerated we are now on the planet. I find in my coaching we are in a time where it is good to look at some of the universal laws and how energy works for some who are waking now and are at the beginning of their healing process. Wherever you are on your journey, it is a good place to explore at this time. Part of the waking up process is to know that you do create your reality and your reality can be unlimited!

85

Universal Laws, Just a Few

The laws of the universe are really no secret at all and have been taught for a very long time. They were never common knowledge to the public so unless you were on the path of awareness you typically would not have come across them. Even then, many forms of teachings to the way of inner awareness never taught much on the universal laws because teachers did not feel that people were ready for them or could accept the concepts. I was lucky in the way that I had many teachers in my life not only teaching me them verbally but many times displaying actions to validate their truth. Even though I was exposed to these truths for many years, it still took me a long time to embrace them into my life. We are open to what we are ready to remember. I say remember, because we always had this knowledge inside of us, we just forgot, we bought into illusions and bought into separateness from Source. There are many Universal Laws at work but I will only cover a few here, and go into some detail about them and how to start applying them as great tools for your journey of healing and living more joyfully.

A.) All and everything in the universe is ENERGY

Think of everything as energy: money, food, your thoughts, your time etc. Many people have a difficult time believing that all is energy. You may want to look at other examples to assist your mind to stretch in this area. Air is every-where, yet you cannot see it, but it is there. In many writings, you hear God is everywhere and in everything, and many religions are based on this, yet you do not see it. When you believe in it, you can imagine and know all the ways God is working through things and people. If you have been saved from a fatal accident you may say, God maneuvered that plan. When you are stranded somewhere, and unexpectedly someone shows up and helps you, you may say God sent you an angel in a human body. So you do see how God works through events and people. Therefore, whether you want to call it Source, God, or energy, the point is most people know and feel a FORCE is at hand. So just for imaginations sake, try and picture everything being energy. You will have to find within yourself what you truly believe on this, but for the sake of getting some points clearly expressed in this book, I will be working from the concept that ALL is energy.

B.) The law of accountability. Realizing you choose what you experience in life, maybe not how you experience it, but whether your experiences are more joyful or less joyful. Everything we have experienced is something we attracted to ourselves from choices we made. Now the big one here is also choice of lessons we chose to learn as soul coming here to experience the human journey.

Many people say, "But I never chose to experience the things that happened in my relationship." You may not have chose the WAY things occurred, but somewhere down the line, you made a choice that put you in the scenario with this person, good or not. In saying that, many who are in negative relationships now, if they looked back, there were always some signs of that dysfunction there, but you chose to ignore it or you believed you could change and make the person different. Now, you may not have chosen that this person maybe two years later has hit you, yet you did make a choice to be with the person even when there were signs in the past of other unhealthy behavior. I can go into so many scenarios where we can see where we chose something and it is why we are living what we are in our now, but as we go along with accountability in the book, I am sure you will have an AHA moment and understand it better in your own personal situations.

C.) Energy follows intent (thoughts, feeling)

Wherever your ATTENTION is, so is YOUR INTENTION.

Where your attention is your intention is and is what will manifest in your life. You focus on lack, you receive lack, you focus on joy, and you receive joy.

Where is Your Attention?

Every individual has their own soul path and soul lessons to learn, so I can't say here on a broad level what you have or haven't done, but I can make a statement of what I have found with the many people I work with or that I coach. The common thread has been people who really believed they had finished what they needed to release, but it is not just about what you let go of; the work is changing your foundation, changing your thoughts and programs and also how you perceive what is happening around you. It is about being in tune with Spirit all around you and seeing, hearing and experiencing Spirit in and through you. Experiencing Spirit takes practice, yes practice. Learning to watch the messages and to remember to go inside and ask, to make sure your inner being is not feeling chaotic and in survival mode when you ask these things. Many people believe that if they just turn their thoughts into positive thoughts it will all turn around, if they just walk away from the old and then sit and wait for the new, it will appear! That would be nice, but if it worked that simply, we would all be lined up outside the triple violet arches of the fast spiritual awakening line to pick up our happy meals and move forward.

Doing the work is really about seeing through the eyes of Spirit and seeing all, as spirit would interpret it. To do that we have to be in our hearts, open hearts. Therefore, first we work on opening our hearts and working on all layers of the heart, the more we do this, the more we automatically see things through the eyes of spirit. Once we do this, we perceive our world, situations around us and even obstacles differently. We see things as learning, as a gift, as an opportunity to grow!

I read a story about a woman who wished to go out of country and she wished to work with higher spiritual people. Her stepmother got very sick and she was dying of cancer and wanted her to come and stay with her until she passed. The woman could have said things like this; "what did I do wrong, how come my manifesting isn't working, I thought positive so why is this happening to me, why is the universe doing this to me?" (I hear these often when something doesn't happen in the way someone wants it to.) Instead, this woman took it as something else she needed to do right now and she knew there would be many lessons and growth in assisting her stepmother. The whole time she helped her stepmother, she never felt resentful or bitter, and she saw everyday as growth and closeness in her heart. Soon after her stepmother passed, she was given the money to take her trip and everything she wanted came to follow. Many say they are walking and living in sprit, yet when things do not come as fast as they want or how they want it, they put blinders on to what Spirit is really saying or showing them. Ego thinks something is wrong, Spirit sees an opportunity at play and growth coming from the experience.

Don't get me wrong, I am human and I throw tantrums when things SEEM to always be going wrong, but I get my tantrum out so I can vent out the human emotion, then I go inside and start doing the inner work. I begin to ask what I need to see, hear and know from my situation and to assist me in being open and receptive enough to get it clearly. It does not mean everyone has to walk this path; no one has to do anything. However, if you say to the universe you want to be your true heart and soul, or you ask the universe (God, Goddess, angels, guides) to show you truth, to assist you to walk your highest path, but then all of your actions and thoughts are opposite that, you will manifest chaos in your life. It is like saying you want a blue car with a stick shift, and then going out shopping and looking at all the red automatics. Conflicting and confusing energies will bring you conflicting and confused results in your life. If the spiritual path seems too hard, then choose a different path, or a different spiritual belief system. The universe does not judge whether you learn it in this lifetime or another, each lifetime is just a drop in the ocean, time is irrelevant.

Manifesting Results

I hear from many people that they have definitely put positive thoughts, passion and excitement towards manifesting a new job, and yet produce no results. Then when I talk with them longer and ask questions, it is in the same breath they tell me they took old and disliked jobs just to make money (doubt) and that they felt depressed and frustrated on it taking too slow to happen. Now, it is the energy of depression, doubt, and frustration that ACTUALLY went out to the universe and it is what magnetized back an outcome. When I read their energies, I find they never really had the true deep down knowing that their dreams would come true, and this is usually because they are not feeling the full power and love of the universe yet. The way to feel this is NOT just to have positive thoughts and hopes they might come true, it is to tune into Spirit, then get to know Spirit to the level you feel and see it in everything, you KNOW Spirit's love and power. This takes a commitment to spend time with exercises to get more and more in tune with Spirit and with your own inner Being, heart, and soul!

Ask yourself, how much time do you spend on focusing on your body, asking it what it wants to tell you, what it needs to be healthy? Ask yourself, how much time do you spend on feeling and talking with your heart, your feelings? How much time do you spend listening to your inner self, your guides, and/or angels? In all the books you have read, all the seminars you have attended, the workshops or lectures you have been to, how often do you use the tools you have learned from them? I do not mean for a week or month after the workshop or book, I mean all the tools you have gathered and learned over your lifetime, how many and how often do you use them in your daily life? Do you sit down daily or weekly and ask is there anything in my life right now that is not healthy for me that I need to let go of? Am I walking in the right direction to manifest my dreams? If not, what do I need to know and do to have my dreams? If I am going in the right direction, what steps would be best for me to take right now to continue to manifest my dreams? If you have a hard time hearing your inner guidance, ask the universe to bring you the message in a way you will hear it and recognize it as your answer. Do not underestimate how the universe works or the power of it, Source uses many things, people, and ways to bring it to you. The universe cannot do so until you ask though, and then you must know inside yourself it will deliver, and then be open to receiving it.

The real way to make a better year for yourself and to see yourself actually manifest more of your heart's desire is to get more in touch with yourself and the universe, not practicing more affirmations or forcing your thoughts to be positive. If you are in synch with Spirit, your thoughts will be there. Here is an evaluation sheet I sent to all of my clients to help them be focused for the first six months of this year, I am adding the exercise here in hopes it may assist you too.

Evaluation of Self/Moving Forward

A) Write a small paragraph of where you are now in these areas of your life, and where you want it to be in **6 months time**.

1) Your spiritual growth/inner growth finding inner peace, joy, and abundance.
2) Your career (what you want to be doing).
3) Realistically, the amount you want to be making monthly.
4) Your relationship with who you are with, or attaining one.
5) Relationships with friends, co-workers etc.
6) How your home looks and feels.
7) Social time, fun time or free time.
8) Physical body/health.

B) What areas do you feel your biggest blocks are right now?

C) What are you willing to do to move past those blocks?

D) List the tools you feel you know you have right now to make changes in your life, whether you are using them or not. Then rate how often you DO use them in daily life.

Tools you have now	Rating

E) On a scale 1 to 10, (10 being highest) how much do you stop and notice daily what Spirit is saying to you, and are you conscious of everyday lessons?

F) How often do you monitor and catch self-sabotaging thoughts and change them immediately, use the 1 to 10 scale.

G) If you had to pick ONE thing to focus on right now that would make you feel at peace, what would that be? Being rich isn't it folks, dig deeper! :)

H) Close your eyes, take deep breaths, and get quiet inside, now write down the one thing Spirit wants to say to you this very moment!

After taking good inner time to answer these questions, take the largest block you think you have and ask inside what you can do, or where you can get the answer to being able to transmute this block. Then look at your list of tools and see if any of these may assist you with this transformation. Then take the answer to G and write five things you can do to get to that goal. Then work on one a week.

Ask yourself truthfully, what you are willing to do and not to do, to reach your highest potential. What truthfully are you willing to choose to do? Be honest with yourself, and if you find you are not willing to do certain things to attain your highest potential, do not beat yourself up, it means there is still some fear in this area. So instead, identify the fear, and work on the fear first.

An example: I had a client that wrote down she wanted to be married to her true mate. But every time we said the word marriage or her true mate and spiritual equal, she would tense up. Well, of course she is not going to manifest this if it makes her tense. We looked at what that meant to her to have her true mate. She saw it as work, he would be her mirror, she would have to look more deeply at herself, and she was not sure she could handle that on a daily basis or that she was ready for that. Well that is ok and a better place to work from because she now knows the real issue. So, instead we focused from a different angle. Her new passion to manifest was worded more like this: I ask to bring in healthy men to my life that I can be friends with, hang out with, and learn from. This felt more comfortable for her and her body and emotional self lit up and was lighter. Now she most likely will call this in because she feels open to receiving it at this level. Layers people, layers!

Pay attention to how your body feels and your breathing, (are you holding it?) how your gut feels and if there is any discomfort, and then look at the fear. Work from there, ask to manifest something more comfortable, but in the same line, as it will teach you layer by layer to open and be able to receive more in steps. I bet if you go over your New Year's resolutions and read them one by one and pay attention to how your body and emotions react, you will find some would be better to rewrite. If you truly want these things in your life, you will be willing to take the little steps and make your way up to the highest level of it. I hope these tips and the questionnaire help you to become clearer on your dreams and your intentions and will assist you to transmute any doubt or fear energies.

It is good to go back periodically and re-evaluate your manifesting and intentions. It is also very important that you remember to acknowledge what you do manifest and express gratitude.

To re-evaluate where you are and where you want to be, try this exercise:

Make a list of all the beliefs you DO have about life. They might be that you deserve to be happy, have a loving relationship, a house in the country, a job you love. You believe in truth, compassion, understanding others, being without ego, for just a few examples. Then ask yourself, which ones are you living now? Which ones are you working on (taking action) and which ones are you just waiting to come to you? Then meditate on it and ask for assistance in seeing what steps you can take right now to manifest these dreams and be living your truths. Embracing those truths and taking action on those truths. Take one of your truths like believing in understanding and compassion. Then look and evaluate your everyday life and note in what areas you may not actually live this truth all the time. Are there certain topics or living experiences you have a difficult time being compassionate about? Can you always express your truths or do you still live in fear with some people, places, or situations that you would not share what you truly believe in? Look in all these areas of your life and look at where you can take action so you can embrace who you are and own who you truly are! If your actions are not in harmony with what you believe then your actions are telling you where your intention really is.

> Make sure you also recognize the ones you are walking, owning, and choosing right now. Give yourself a pat on the back and honor yourself for already working through those and for the work and growth you have achieved. Be kind to yourself in this exercise and be honest with yourself.

Keep a journal and write down how you are doing on the steps to take that you have chosen. Pay attention and see if any of the steps you are using need to be modified or changed. Many times, we have made progress on things in our lives and they occurred so subtly that we do not even know we have grown into them already. This is where a journal really helps. Meditate often, listen and act on your guidance and do not be fearful to be yourself wherever you are. Spend time in nature for it is very calming and nature is a great place to hear your inner guidance differently. The outdoors is very healing and soothing. Do not forget Spirit is in all and guidance comes through nature and animals too. Pay attention to all the messages around you and realize that when you live awake and aware, life is magickal.

The Difference between Affirmations and Intention

We have all read information over the years about affirmations and how they help us think positive and create what we want. Yet, many people in my classes over the years ask, why it is not working for them? I would not say the technique does not work at all, because I think by saying affirmations they help you to remember to think more positively. After years with experience teaching workshops, I have found that people have not manifested much JUST by saying affirmations.

To manifest things you want in life, and I don't mean like a TV unless that is what your goals are, I mean a happier and more abundant life, abundant not just in money, but in love, joy, harmony and such, you need the following:

> Truly desire it.
> Feel worthy of it.
> Know you deserve it.
> Be able to receive.

Thought creates and creating can only be in energy form, then it takes emotion plus desire to manifest it into the physical. All manifestations come from the emotional energy (how strong we feel it inside) behind your intent.

Example: If you are saying an affirmation everyday: I want more joy, love, and money, and you just keep saying this everyday and focusing on it, yet you have thoughts about yourself such as: It is bad to want money, I am not good enough, and I feel uncomfortable inside when I receive things from people.

Then your affirmation is I want more love, joy and money in my life, but YOUR INTENTION is I really can't or don't feel comfortable receiving. So, you get the latter. No matter how much you think you really want the affirmation, the words have become emotionless, the intention of lack of receiving or worthiness is the stronger emotion, which will be your true intent (unconsciously) and that is what will manifest.

The only way you are going to have what you truly want in a life is to work on yourself inside, change how you see things in the world, and learn to love yourself. We come with a huge truckload of programs such as things have to be hard, things are drama, and these programs came through experiences we had in our life. Our subconscious then files them as a program, we experienced them, and so it has logged it as a truth about life. The idea is to WAKE UP, and remove the programs, create better experiences in life, and then see how we can change the tapes of the programs to a different idea of life.

However, it is NOT done from just thinking positive thoughts; it is working inside yourself to change your programming, and to manifests new truths about life. Like erasing a hard drive and starting to load new programs, positive ones:)

Many times when someone (not always) stays in Trauma Drama and negativity all the time, it is a distraction, it gives that person an excuse not to have to be accountable of self, do the hard work, and change inside. It distracts us from working on ourselves and of having to see ourselves. This is ok, if this is what a soul wants, but then it becomes the choice of other people (souls) to decide if they want to keep participating in that soul's drama to the point that it distracts them from their own inner work. The coolest thing about earth, it is a place of freedom of choice as a soul, and in everyday and every moment we can make a different choice.

Create Intentions Daily

It is good to create intentions daily; this assists you in staying focused on what you would like to have your attention on during the day. It helps keep your thoughts positive and your eye on the goal.

Here are some things you can ask for as an intention for the day:
To hear my guides/angels better today
For more clarity today
Help me see signs and understand them today
Abundance (clarify) in all things, just joyful things, love, money, otherwise you could get JUST abundance of anything
Peace, Calm
More time to yourself
Assist me to get clearer on what my passion is
Intention could be, understand your intuition more today
Call laughter to yourself, Lighten up the day

Intentions I can set for the day!

Based on new choices you want to make, write your goal in the center of the flower, and then write your intentions in the petals that *will* your goals. Like Stress free for the goal, intention is focus on calm; intention is for smooth day etc.

A Daily Routine—Moving Meditation

Each morning as you shower, you can say, I wash away all negativity, all worries, doubts and fears down the drain. I call into this day the intention to manifest all abundance, success, and opportunities that are for my higher good and the highest good of all. (This way you do not limit what comes to you) I always say manifest because if you are always creating, then it could stay in the creative stage and not become manifest in the physical.

Then during the day when fear, worries, and doubt come up, keep a small tablet with you, and write the opposite down of the thought. I find taking a physical action assists much more than trying to fight the thought.

Example: If the thought pops up, I will never get that deal (work deal) write down all you would do with the abundance that would come from that deal, such as get a house, helps so and so.

More on Intention for the Day

Here is a fun one to play with. Every morning I send out an intention for my day, but you do not want it to be too detailed because then you limit what can come to you. An example would be; I state, I am sending the intent for more calm and peace today, or I am sending the intent for abundance today, then maybe I will add financial abundance.

If you start little don't be disappointed, the more you acknowledge what you receive the more that will come, so let's say I say More financial abundance today, and I find a five dollar bill on the ground, I say I am grateful for this abundance and it is now tripling. GET IT?

Another good one for the day is I send the intent today to call to me a new friend, or a new opportunity in my life, and do not give up, say it every day until you get it.

Now reach for the stars! Write in the stars below your wildest dreams you want to manifest. Have fun and do not limit your imagination.

Keys to Like Attracts Like

- Working with a Mirror Concept
- Everyone and Everything in Our Life Are Reflections of an Aspect of Our Being at Some Time
- We Reflect Our Inner Being in Our Environment by What We Attract
- Interpreting Your Home and Vehicle as Aspects of Your Being

Like Attracts Like or Law of Attraction

I first learned this from a Kahuna (Hawaiian Shaman) who worked with me on my spiritual growth. After many years of learning this one and then learning to always be aware of it in my life, I then in turn have taught it in my workshops and in my coaching for many years. This concept is referred to in many ways, like attracts like, or mirrors in your life. Many people seem to have a difficult time applying this one in their lives because their ego gets loud and they do not have discernment of what the mirror is. This is because the mirror can seem to work as attracting exactly what you think you are and also it can seem to mirror the opposite, so many are not sure what it is they own inside when first working with this concept. I usually come up with many different exercises for people to do depending on who they are and where they are on their journey because to me hands on is the best way to truly GET IT!

Like Attracts Like

Everyone and everything in our life is a mirror reflection of something inside of us. Past, present and future. One person might mirror where we have already been, something we have already healed and moved past, while another can mirror what we own inside right now, what we are going through in our present moment, and another could be the future, what we own inside but do not yet know that we do. Some can carry one or more mirrors for us.

Examples: If something irritates you about someone, it means you own something inside yourself and what you are feeling irritated about is mirroring something to you. It is being mirrored to you so that you can see it, work on it, and heal it. The mirror is not always how the other person is displaying it in their life, but more what the issue is. For instance, at a time in my life when I was working with politicians, my concept of them was that they were people who lied and hid things and they were not in integrity. I felt stumped at the universe as I thought of it back then when in reality my own higher self put me in this mirror, this can't

100

be right? Because I thought I hated anything to do with lying or being deceptive I knew I did not own those qualities inside of me and I strive to be the opposite of those things, so how could this be a mirror? Ask, and you will always receive the answer. On meditating and working with my inner voice and my teachers, it was pointed out to me that even though I was not acting it out as they did, I still owned the same issues they did. I have judgment about them, hmmm, yet I believed they were judgmental of others. I was out of integrity with myself back then in my life because I was doing work I hated but did it because I needed the money to raise my kids, yet I believed and spoke to others about being in the work they truly love and trusting. Where some of the politicians were out of integrity with others, I was out of integrity with myself. Doesn't make anyone right or wrong where they were on their journey, it was just mirrors of what we own inside.

Now if you asked me if I was nonjudgmental and living my truths, I would have said yes and truly believed that. This is why the mirrors can help, when you are in a situation that is "talking to you," then it is trying to show you something you need to see that you may not be aware of about yourself at the time. If it keeps reflecting itself to you, you will eventually see it. On the other side of this, I can only magnetize to myself (like attracts like) what I truly am inside, NOT what I think I am. I was seeing mirrors of what were truly still subconscious issues and this tool assisted me to bring it to light, into the conscious state so I could work with it.

There was a time when I was working with many clients that had a problem with lying, or people lying to them in their lives. I also know from my walk in this journey, that if you are being visited by a common theme, even if you are working with others with this issue, it is probably trying to talk to you also. Mirrors work in different ways; it is sort of like the mirrors in a fun house. Some look normal, some make you look skinny, fat, or distorted, but they are all still mirrors, you may have to just really look at what angle or aspect that particular mirror is reflecting to you. When I had the theme occurring with the clients that had the lying occurring in their lives, I had to say to myself, ahhhh, raising the green flag, yes green not red, I have my own flags to what they mean to me, and green is time to look and heal something and grow. I will explain at the end of the chapter. I then looked within and asked my higher self, what is it I need to see and know within me where lying is an issue? I found that I was unconsciously lying to myself about certain areas of my life, thinking I had worked through them when indeed there were more layers to heal. They presented themselves and I worked with them and healed them. When we are paying attention to the mirrors in our lives, we can always know or ask where we need healing. Therefore, a common theme that keeps showing itself to you in life is usually always a message to pay attention and look inside.

Here is a different angle on the lesson with mirrors: At one time in my life, I was hanging out with nothing but Shamans, Kahuna, and other teachers of the spiritual. They pointed out to me, they were a mirror of what I own inside and some day would be teaching like they were because it was who I was inside (meaning I had the same information they did), yet still unconsciously. They pointed out to me they were my mirror for what I owned inside and still needed to find within me. I always loved how my teacher Jay would say yes; GURU is exactly what it says, Gee You Are You! Pointing out that we all own that Master inside of us whether we are consciously aware of it or not.

When you call these mirrors into your life of things you own but do not know you do yet, then they are a message to you that you are ready to go to the next step and it is coming to you soon. Mirrors take practice, but if you learn to be more aware of them, you will always know what you need to work on inside, what you need to change, and what may be your next step.

Taking a little review here, since all is energy, all energy follows intent, and like attracts like, and this works in all parts of your life. People are not just mirrors; mirrors can be found in nature, in animals and so forth, just pay attention. Everything in your life is magnetized to you, because it is the law of attraction, and since all is energy all forms of energy attracts itself to itself. Sound confusing? It isn't really.

Things that stand out to you during the day are messages. During each day, there are always one or more things that really grab our attention, which I call, "energy is talking to you". Even if you think this is crazy or way out there, what can you lose by trying it? Play with it and see what you find out. It goes with the same concept of your house representing you, whatever is really going on in your house, decor, clean, or cluttered, this is what is mirroring how you feel and are in the moment inside yourself.

Do this exercise in your home right now and let us see how much of it is a reflection. I have been using this exercise for over fourteen years with my clients and students and they are always amazed at how accurate it is.

Walk around your home with a pad of paper and pen, and write down in each room what is in there and what it means to you. Let us start with the kitchen, is it clean and spacey, or is it cluttered? Are your pots and pans or dishes in a way that is easily accessible? How much food is in the cupboards and in the refrigerator and what kind of food is it, healthy, junk or comfort foods? Do you have dishes or foods in the kitchen you will never use or eat but hang on to them? What color is your kitchen? What is your floor like?

Let us just start with this for now. I will make up a scenario and give an example of what this might mean and reflect to someone if their kitchen was like this: The walls are yellow but with old paint and have not been cleaned in a while. The floor is linoleum and in good shape but the person does not like it because she wants to have a stone tile floor. Her pots are old but functional yet she dislikes cooking with them. She has many canned and frozen leftovers she has not touched in a long time and does not really plan to eat. There is some healthy food and some junk food.

Taking everything as symbolic let us put some meanings here. Let us assume the kitchen is symbolic of how we take spiritual food in, spiritual information and how we take in this knowledge to grow.

The floor being foundation, then the floor of a kitchen is spiritual foundation, and then the yellow represents mental and being in our power. She does not like the floor so she probably wishes her spiritual life was different, a more strong and different foundation. She had or has a good enough foundation but it does not seem to fit her anymore, it is not the one she truly wants.

Let us take the food; she has healthy and junk food, and food she will never eat. She has some knowledge and information on her awareness path that is good information and some she just acquired on her journey, and then she still has some that she does not believe in but has never released even though they really are not her truths. This information could be from friends, family, beliefs growing up and books that she has read. Her kitchen is telling her symbolically that she needs to sit and sift through all the information she has about spiritual and find what truly feels right for her and release the rest. The information she may not be too sure on yet, she needs to still shift through. She probably finds herself mentally processing those that no longer really fit her or that she no longer wants. Her pots and pans represent that her spiritual tools seem to be functioning in a mediocre fashion, but she has no tools that are inspiring growth or change. She feels her tools are old and outgrown and she does not see other tools available at this time.

Now this is just a general overview of things, it would go much deeper if we added all the rooms in the house and who else lives in the house. However, it is a great tool to play with to validate how much like attracts like and how much your surroundings will teach you about yourself and others in the family. Play with this and do not judge any of it, just view it as a mirror and what it is trying to say to you and what you may want to change in your life.

Here is a symbolic map for you to play with and use. See what wonderful explorations about yourself you will make, and also to help you understand how many different ways mirrors work and how the law of attraction works in many different ways.

Some Symbols

The key and secret is to pay attention, and to learn the right questions to ask in our lives. Here are just a few meanings to the larger areas in our lives that reflect to us. You must also take the MAIN symbol and then apply what is happening with it to make the story of yourself.

Remember that by the time you have manifested these messages in your outer world, they have been talking to you a long time and you have not been listening. Now they are screaming!

House Your house, or if you are living with someone, your living space, represents your spiritual self. So, whatever is going on in your house will reflect what is happening to you on a spiritual level.

Attics are your higher self.

Main floor is your everyday spiritual issues or growth.

Basements are your blocks or your deepest fears.

Bathrooms represent your cleansing, releasing, detoxing, or not dealing with issues such as backed up plumbing.

Bedrooms are intimacy and relationship with self or a mate.

Stairs represent your direction in life and whether it is strong or not.

Doors and windows are opportunities to open to higher Self. Doors would be walking in a new direction or next step in life; windows are more about opening to wisdom and guidance.

Office space in the home is business.

Game rooms are the fun and joy in life.

Dining rooms are about sitting and accepting spiritual food in your life.

Kitchens are wanting spiritual food in your life.

Garage is where you store info and tools you need in life. Therefore, if the garage is holding many items to your past you are holding on to the past things in your spiritual that you no longer need and do not apply to your new self and life. No room to bring new info for the new you in.

Living room is about family, closeness, relationships, and social activity.

Closets are things we hide away and remember only when things are triggered.

Backyards are about nurturing self, growing, planting new ideas, blossoming, tuning into nature and that aspect of spirit.

So, let us look at some things that may be happening. Ask your self these questions:

How is the plumbing in the house?

Look around each room and see if it is cluttered, dusty, too organized (uncomfortable to be self in).

How are the doors and windows, shut, stuck, can't close, jammed?

Check the walls for holes.

How do you feel in each room? Do you hurry through it, feel safe and warm, comfortable etc?

Changing your outer world to what you want to be your inner space puts a strong energy out to the world that you are bringing this new energy in. So cleaning things up and out will start to bring this to your own life. Remember the law of attraction.

Many times while we are working on the outer part of the house we will go through our emotions and what we are letting go of, and in a more joyful way we will be processing at the same time. This is why when you change to what you want to call in, attract it into your life, it works, and you still did the inner work. It works, TRUST ME!

Start with just one area in your life so you do not self-sabotage yourself by feeling overwhelmed. When you get comfortable with this then move on to the next exercises below and eventually use this tool in every waking moment as your out walking about in the world while being aware of things "that talk to you".

Vehicles, the one you use the most as yours will reflect what is going on with your physical body. There are too many to list here but we will cover the most obvious here.

Gas is the fuel we put in our body, as in food and the amount. (Do you wait until your car is empty before refueling)? If so, then this is what you also do to your body, waiting too long between meals and rest and waiting until you have no more energy before you put fuel in and rest.

Electrical is your energy and what is happening to your energy. Are you over energetic to the point of shorts, or are you killing your battery (not rejuvenating)?

Warning lights on in your car will tell you about organs in your body. Depends on the warning light message.

Do you forget and leave your emergency brake on when driving? This is you wanting to move forward in life but a part of you is sabotaging that due to a fear you are holding on to.

Does your car need a tune up? Do you need a check up?

Do you check all the fluids before they get low enough to tell you about it?

Do you take care of your body before it gets to discomfort to let you know it needs attention?

Is the outer body of the vehicle in shape? Are you taking care of your outer body too?

Car accidents depending on where the car is hit and how will determine the issue you are carrying.

Remember that if you share a vehicle or a house it also reflects issues of the others involved but will also affect you. If you're sharing space with someone it is a soul agreement to learn these lessons with them, so there may be two different lessons but they will apply to both of you or however many of you.

List things in your car and house that would be reflecting an issue now or is still holding old energy of who you were and NOT who you are now!

Part and/or item in car or house:	Reflecting the issue …

Flags

Now about the green flag I mentioned earlier in this chapter. I feel we should have fun walking our path, even when working on issues. In meditation, I will set up a language for myself and what it means to me, and then from that day on I just call the image and know what I am putting intent to. I chose this tool because when ego is talking in a negative way we tend to use the tools in a less than way, like oops, ego be quiet, or oops, I had a thought of lack warning. This way with my flags, I made a language in the more positive direction of communicating with the inner self. An example would be that when I think lack, instead of saying a warning to myself, I will say, green flag, heal this, and bring in abundance.

I made the language of my flags, when I see a mirror in the moment, I will say oh, raising the _____ flag. This is a reminder to myself to get back to it in my meditation and what it is I am getting back to, since I have made different meanings to my different flags. I have many things in life I do this with; it makes the journey fun, interesting and provides tools.

Choose your own symbology and meanings but I will list my flags here in case you would like to use this tool.

Red Flag = Time to birth, move to the next level.
Green Flag = Time to heal and grow.
Orange Flag = Time to create or be creative.
Blue Flag = Time to look at the deeper truth of things, see through illusions.
Pink = Time to go deeper into the heart.
Fuchsia = Transformation.
Brown= Earthy and time to go inside to hibernate.
Violet = Time to see a bigger vision.
Silver = Re-evaluate what I am reflecting out to the world.
Gold = Re-evaluate what I am manifesting in my world right now.
Yellow = Reflect on am I walking in my power and am I assisting others to walk in their power.

After meditating on your meanings, color your flags and write in the meaning that color or symbol you have chosen means to you.

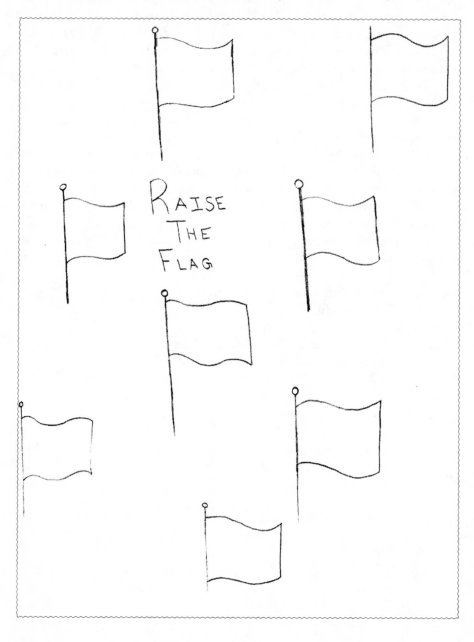

Write in the magnets what you want to attract to you in life.

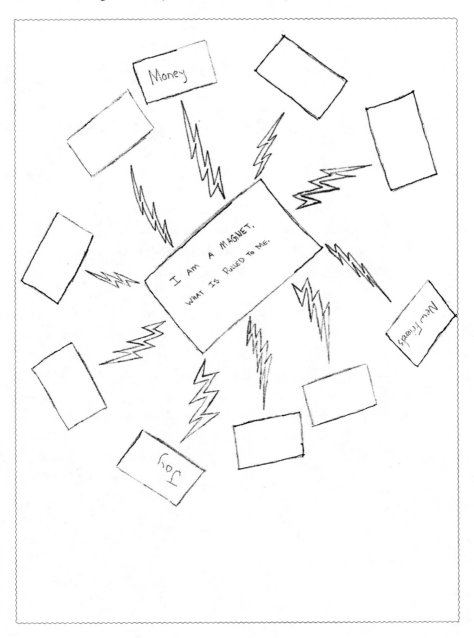

Keys to the Balance of Things

- Balancing All Areas of Our Life, One at a Time
- Did You Work Things Out or Did You Shift the Focus?
- Balance Is the Key at This Time of Accelerated Shifting

The Balance of Things

Another of the universal laws is Balanced Rhythmic Interchange. The universe and energy works on balance, so if we are out of balance in one area of our life, other areas will in turn be out of balance.

The focus will be on integrating our newfound selves and our new energies by living more in the positive. We will learn to manifest balance. We need to find balance in all parts of our lives, but we cannot do that in every aspect at once. We need to focus on one part at a time and make a process of the changes we seek.

It is important to first look at all the areas of our life and take note where we are out of balance. The way we eat and health consciousness, habits, work, and yes even where our main focus is everyday. If anything is in lack, we are out of balance. If we are doing things or focusing on anything in the extreme, this is being out of balance. Let's say, for example, we used to be a workaholic and we make a change to make sure we have more social time, but then end up planning so much social time that our calendar is as busy as before when we were the workaholic. Many times we trick ourselves into thinking we made a healthy change. It becomes an illusion that we are in balance or have worked on the issue. The same issue exists; as in the example stated, it could be that we have a difficult time spending time alone with ourselves, or we have to be busy to fill a void and make us feel productive and worthy. Changing from one extreme to another will only make it *seem* like we have truly made change. We find balance when we make sure the changes are about finding why we do something in the extreme first, and then making healthy choices that assist us in having a well-rounded life.

Physical Balance

Let us look at health. We cannot continue to push our bodies too hard and keep a poor diet, not get enough rest, and then not really see that eventually our body will tell us about it by becoming ill. Just as we can have the lack of what our body needs out of balance, I would like to look at another form of being out of balance with the body. I have read about and worked with many people over the years in the healing field that have gone to the extremes in staying in what they believe, is a healthy state. Many have been out of balance by making sure their bodies are so clean and pure that it actually causes imbalances. They made sure every-thing they ate was low or had NO chemicals, all natural and organic, had regular cleanses and purification, and used almost all alternative medicines (herbs). What has happened in the last two years is now these people, for one reason or another, have had to resort to western drugs or treatment. Because their bodies were so cleansed and protected from many of the chemicals in this world, they had no built-up resistance to them. The result is that they have become much more ill requiring a longer recovery. Having all chemical free foods and beverages, doing regular cleanses and staying as natural as possible sounds very healthy. I am not saying it is not a good thing to be health conscious. However, when it is lived to the extreme it is still not balanced. Many of these friends or clients made sure for the last fifteen years or more that they eliminated all foods and chemicals from their environment that were known to cause cancer, yet still manifested cancer in their bodies. For them, the emotional pain has been just as debilitating as the disease because they were so sure that their cautionary measures would keep them at a very low, or no risk rate. Again, we need to find the balance and many times what we think is the best is an illusion. We have to work on the fears and issues that actually manifest dis-ease in the body. If we don't, all the health diets in the world will not work to prevent us from these dis-eases. Let us say we focus ninety percent on the physical, then that leaves only ten percent left to focus on other areas of our lives.

Spiritual Balance

Now let us look at our spiritual aspect. We can focus so much on our higher spiritual self that we also become out of balance. The BIG lesson here is to be a spiritual being in a body, and it is important to balance it with our mundane life. One example of this would be a woman I observed two months ago. She is a well-known healer and intuitive. She had a near death experience and when she recovered, she found she had increased healing and psychic abilities. She went out to teach to the world to be grateful for every moment and live your dream. She started a healing church and has 250 to 300 attendees every week. I was listening to a talk she was giving to a group and I noticed that her physical body was suf-fering, and as I tuned into her, she had many issues in her emotional body as well. Yet, she was definitely channeling a clear and higher knowledge. Her talk was great, but it was clear she had not worked on balance herself in her own body. In talking with another healer there of what I observed, she said she had worked with this woman and there were signs that her body was burning out. The woman told her she was only concerned and almost obsessed with higher spiritual teachings and knowledge and wanted to be as open as possible. However, the healer/intuitive was ignoring her own body and its messages to her. She was teaching others to be awake and alive yet she was skipping meals and ignoring her own needs for rest by constantly traveling and not taking time out to rest or rejuvenate. Because of this, it had caused her body to be out of balance. It is literally frying and shutting down many physical organs. She truly believed that she needed only to concern herself with spiritual teaching and getting the message out there. While she has abundance in that area of her life, her everyday life is in a lot of lack. She complains there is a lack of help and support from others, she financially struggles, and her energy is given away to others to the point she has none left for herself. Many would think or say that as long as we are being helpful to others and doing the spiritual work, the mundane does not matter. Yet, how spiritual can we be if we abuse our own lives and body on a daily basis? How can we teach others to love themselves when we do not love our own self? We are meant to be healthy, happy, and abundant in these bodies and doing so does not make us any less spiritual, it means we are walking in spirit.

Mental Balance

We can be caught up in the mental as well. We can process so much that we regurgitate our thoughts until they no longer make sense or we have lost the meaning of what we were processing to begin with. Our minds can get into so much noise over our fears, doubts and worries that we tune out hearing the voice of our higher self. We can find the balance of our minds by learning to quiet the chatter, to hear and feel the stillness and then we are able to hear our higher self. Even illusions of mentally processing our spiritual messages can occur and turn into mentally beating the message to death. We can be so stuck in our head trying to figure out the lessons in our lives that we no longer are participating in the experience of the lessons. We are tricked by the ego that over-processing is exploring our lessons. Balance in this area will be very important because the energies are so accelerated and will continue to be so. We will need this balance to stay centered and clear. With so many things moving at such a fast rate, it is important to be flowing with the wave of energies so we do not feel overwhelmed and caught up in the illusions that we face in the world.

There are so many changes happening on the earth and the vibrational shifts are so accelerated it is creating many changes in each of our lives whether we feel we are ready for them or not. The best way to ride this wave and feel the balance is to start in your own homes and your own lives. Like never before we will all need a place we go to where there is calm and harmony, a sanctuary that we have created with our own personal energies. Many people create a personal altar of what they are working on or what they want to manifest in their life in a special space.

Some create a corner of one room to start changing the whole room. Eventually every place in your own home should be a place of calm and harmony. Start with a small space and let it grow with you as you embrace the changes. Let your intuition lead you through this process as your intuition will be growing and changing too.

As time passes we will become much more aware of how interconnected we all are on the planet, with the planet and beyond. Our intuitions are increasing. As our vibrations rise, we will become more and more sensitive to negative energy around us. Many will feel that they can no longer stay too long in an area where the energy is chaotic; we will feel less tolerable at first in these energies. You will crave to be in the calm energies. People will want to be more in nature and have a need to do so more often. What will help during these adjustments is to read all you can on awareness, attend classes on it, find an exercise such as Yoga or Tai Chi. Baths or sea salt baths will help to clear out the aura. Play soothing music. Hang out with friends and family that are positive and encouraging. Sit in nature, and/or bring it in by getting small waterfalls with different sounds for different rooms in the house. Surround yourself with colors and smells in your home, car, and office that make you feel good inside. Take walks or drives in scenery you enjoy. Pay attention to signs and ask for guidance and then be open to what the answers are and in all ways the answers are brought to you. Most of all.... BREATHE!!!! Through all of it.

Mirrors and balance can be learned by watching nature. Sometimes mirrors are reflecting opposites and other times it is reflecting similarities. Balance is knowing when to flow with the energies and not try to manipulate the energy to what we think we want. There are times in our life where the best action is no action. It is like winter when all plants rest and rejuvenate, that is going with the flow, yet when humans feel a rest period they think something is wrong. Balance knows when to rest, rejuvenate or when to be energetic and take action. This is flowing with the universe.

Tool on seeing how you can be out of balance:

Make a list, divide paper in half long ways, list in one day EVERY place you put out energy, energy meaning:

How many people do you help a day?
How much time on the phone with others _for_ others daily?
How much time on computer?
How much time with driving or picking up kids etc?
How much time house cleaning?

How much time spent at a job?

How much time with friends and is it social or is it always your helping them?

How much time with all other family members?

When doing this exercise, look at where you are being giving to them even at compromising yourself. (Giving is good when in balance)

Next to each thing you have listed on a scale of one to ten, ten being the highest, how much energy are you expending?

Then on the other side of the paper, write how much energy you receive daily, and I do not mean, joy from helping someone, actual receiving from another.

How much time is for you in pampering you, or doing something special for you, or letting someone else help you or delegating chores or errands? List all of those on the other side of your divided page. If the list labeled "out" is longer than then the list labeled "in" then your energy account is overdrawn! This will catch up with you, as there are always overdraft fees, BIG! If you are doing this many times a week then your money is also out of balance in your life (back to mirrors), I will bet ya. Point is it is giving the universe the contradictive message you want abundance. If you are always giving out, how can you have room or time to receive? If you do this in one area of your life, it will show itself in other areas as well, such as your money flow. Play with this exercise in other areas of your life.

What does balance look like to me?

Write or draw what balance in your life looks like to you. It could be scales, yin yang symbol, male and female, or a clean house. List or draw, as many symbols as you can think of that are balance to you.

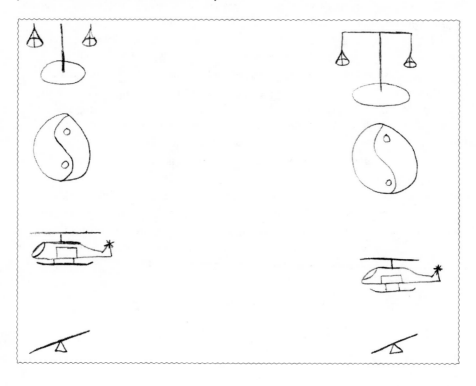

Keys to Soul Purpose/Soul Path

- Actively Learn and Grow Everyday
- There is No One Purpose or Path
- We Are Always Changing as We Learn and Grow
- Do not Limit Your Self
- Ask! Source/Universe Always Answers

Soul Purpose/Soul Path

Most people get caught up in the question of why am I here and what is my purpose? In all truth, we are here to learn and grow, and it does not matter how we do that, just that we do it. Many people believe it is ONE thing we do that is our soul purpose when in reality it is all we do. The ideal way to walk this journey is to be conscious and accountable, but even if someone is asleep or walking the journey unconscious, they are still walking their soul path. Being conscious and accountable is walking it more joyfully and understanding how all that is happening in our life is how we think, which is how we draw lessons to us. Everything that has occurred to us already on this planet is our story, and our story is about how we walked the journey, the journey is the soul path here on the earth. Once we learn that life happens in our story according to our perceptions in life and about life, we can understand where and how we are also accountable.

Thought is the energy tool to create around us and action is what manifests those creations. As we create and manifest we choose to have experiences, and these experiences are what teach us and allow us to become wise. Action leads us to wisdom. We cannot know what a "thing" will become until we act on it. Our experience based on that action is what assists us to become wise. I have many wise moments that came from an OOPS experience, where I have looked back and said, hmm, I could have made a better choice of action. Yet I still learned from the experience, which has made me wiser. I have had other moments where I look back and say; "Damn I am good." Either way I am wiser for them. Where if I made no decisions and took no action, I stay in the "I will never know stage" or the "blaming outside forces in the world for my life."

We all have talents we were born with that we can utilize on our path. Some people get confused by thinking that there is only one soul purpose. We actually have many purposes on our walk here on earth. I will use myself as an example: I have a unique way of seeing the true heart of people often (☺) even before they know it. I have an ability to communicate with many people no matter what their beliefs and I can say things in a manner they will be able to understand. I see solutions to obstacles because for me obstacles are opportunities. I have a bubbly personality that makes others feel better.

Over the course of my journey, I have worked with handicapped children on horseback, and loved it. I worked at Chevron at one time as a keypunch operator and then later as a Lead, yet I touched many people on a personal level because of my kind of interaction with them. I have worked as a healer, a teacher, and a coach for businesses and as a transformational coach, and yet ALL of these were part of my soul path. Why? Because I walked them, I learned from them and most of all I loved doing them. Yet, even back when I was asleep, and I was an over giver with no boundaries, walking my journey from the perception of a person who grew up in a dysfunctional family, lived in survival and so on, I was still on my path. I was walking it unconsciously then, yet still walking it nonetheless, and it was all that pain and dysfunction that made something inside me say, WAKE UP! That something was my ever growing and loud inner voice that was telling me, and reminding me, that things could be different. My journey then was not happy and I wanted to be happy. So my inner voice urged me to want to learn more and seek out how to change my current path, but it was still being on my soul path.

Many people tell me when they hear of all the things that I have experienced in my life that pertain to my soul path that they are amazed and ask how I found all those tools to wake up and change. My answer is I wanted them! It is that simple, and these tools found me, because I drew them to me by just truly wanting them and believing I would find my answers. One important thing I have owned inside since a young child is that I always believed with a strong conviction, if you really want to understand something and really want an answer from God/Source, you would always have it. I learned later in life, you hear that answer when you are ready to hear it. I have studied many ways of spirituality, and been through many layers. Even when I did not have a certain belief system, I always knew Source was with me and I always knew I would be answered.

If you truly want to make your life happier and you want to know the steps you need to take to get there, then just ask, put it out in prayer. If you truly desire it, then the answers to those steps will come to you. It is also helpful to be clear on what you are asking and how you ask it. So, if you are saying, show me my soul purpose, then in every breath you are taking is already the answer. You may want to say, show me what it is in life that I would be happy doing, and that will help others and the planet, then watch for the answer. Or, please guide me to see what I need to change inside of myself so that I can have a happier and healthier life. Again, you must be open to recognizing the answers and have a knowing you will be answered. Many times people say they are not answered, when in reality they are not feeling worthy of an answer. Then it is time to ask, please assist me in loving myself and knowing within me that I am worthy. If you ask this every day, opportunities will come to you that will show you your worth. Many times the answer has come and we were just not paying attention to it.

In my experiences of many beliefs I do know one thing, no matter if people prayed to Buddha, or St. Francis, Mary, Shiva, or White Buffalo Woman, whatever that person called spirit or Source, they all still were answered. I always see it as all the paths lead to the ONE. It is wonderful that apparently Source is not working out of ego, so is not partial to what it is called. After asking what it is you want to be clear on, or that you need help with, then know you will hear or see that answer when you are ready to hear or see it. Many times, I have asked Source to assist me to remove and heal any blocks I have so I can be open to the answer of the highest good.

What do I mean by the highest good?

For me it has more than one meaning. It means the more joyful path, which pretty much sums up all the others. The other meanings for me are the answers to these three questions:

> Will this serve me to be a better person and grow?
> Does this serve others to assist in their growth?
> Is this from love?

A yes answer to those questions is of the highest good. I learned this by asking for things in life thinking what I was asking for was for my best. Then getting them only to find out they were not necessarily the best thing to ask for or I asked for something I thought I wanted which after receiving, found it was not what I truly wanted at all. <chuckle> Hmmm, once again leading to wisdom. There is a great country song called, "God's Greatest Gifts are Unanswered Prayers."

Think of your prayer as your intention. When you ask for clarity, your intention is to receive clarity. Then do we just sit back and wait passively for the answer? Not in my book. I believe it is to always be followed with an action. It could be daily meditating. Also depends on what you are asking for. You may have to actively research things you are asking about, or take a class. The more we ask ourselves and Source for living and walking our soul walk, the more receptive we are to seeing, hearing and recognizing how the answers come for us. I never teach that there is only one way for the answers to come. I always add in my prayer or intention that I ask for the answer in the most joyful way.

When I have a class on helping others get their own answers I do some exercises in class to see how each students' own language works. Some will manifest physical answers, such as a card in the mail, which promotes an AHA moment, and they know it is an answer. Some get answers symbolically, some get it in pieces, which they need to put together like a puzzle to get the bigger picture. No matter how good we get at it, we tend to let the human side out once in awhile and still doubt the answer we get especially if it is a large choice in life. However, keep asking and it will make itself clear to you.

I have walked my life a long time in layers of being open and trusting and I feel I am confident in trusting my answers. Yet when I was offered a wolf for about the seventh time in my life, I was unsure on my answer. People would make the offer not knowing why they were and just offered. When I was studying with a Native American teacher she and many others have told me Wolf is my medicine, meaning I have attributes the same as wolf. Wolf can represent teacher and one who gathers experiences and takes it back to the clan. In all the cases where I was offered a wolf I have said no immediately because I would not raise one in the city. This one particular time I was offered a part wolf part malamute; I actually stopped to think about it. I had decided no. The man who had the mother who had not delivered her pups yet, sent me pictures of them right after they were delivered and also about every week as they grew. I kept thinking about it and wondering if this was a message to get one. I then asked higher self and Source if this is a good thing for me and for the wolf?

After asking, I went on the Internet and looked up information on raising a wolf in the city. None looked too promising. The next day I went out to meditate, driving to a favorite nature place of mine, asking again, why am I even considering this wolf? I wrote in my journal, and still with mixed feelings, I surrendered to Source. I decided that if I were to take this wolf I would get an answer in a big way. When I returned home, there was a small package on my doorstep. I went into the house and opened the card attached to it, it was from a student I had and had not talk to in years, and it said:

> Dear Anne, I am sorry I missed you today. I was in the neighborhood and thought I would bring you this gift. I made it sometime ago but never got around to giving it to you. I hope you like it, I miss you and love you, call me. Rachelle

I opened the gift and staring at me was a face of a wolf in a frame, outlined in leaves. Hmmm, I said to self, is this a big sign. (Now I know better than this, but it shows you how we can test our answers and ourselves) I decided maybe not. I then asked again, "Source let me know without a doubt whether I should take this wolf or not?" Two days later a friend of mine came to see me and said he was cleaning out his storage unit and saw this picture and thought of me so he wanted to give it to me. He handed it to me and it was a picture of a wolf on a wood piece background. Well now, this should have been my sign, but my stubborn self was still not convinced. It was a very big emotional deal for me and I had many reasons to be reluctant to take this wolf. For one I would hate to raise an animal in an environment they hated, two, wolves are pack animals and a lot of work, three I had a seventeen year old lab and she was not quite physically up for a puppy or a wolf.

Since I have this inner language of my own, which is three times and it is so, I decided to tell Source, ok, this might be an answer. But if it is a definite yes to take the wolf, make it three times that I get the answer. A woman who had invited me to a special medicine wheel ceremony in Oregon, which I sadly had to decline as I had a previous engagement but told them I would be there in spirit, later came to visit me. She told me all that attended brought wrapped gifts to put in the center of the wheel, and each person intuitively took a gift from the center when they left. She said since they knew I was there in spirit they put one in for me. This friend intuitively chose a gift from the middle asking that it be for me. I opened it and it was a framed picture of wolf eyes that are normally sold to raise money for saving the wolves.

OK, OK, I GET IT!!!! I then e-mailed the man who offered me the wolf and took my dear and now best friend, Takota. Six months after I took him my dear friend Roxanne, my seventeen and a half year old lab passed away. It seemed that all of it was in divine order and meant to be and I was so happy I had taken Takota. His name means friend to all and he is. Everyone who meets Takota is shocked he is seventy-five percent wolf, for he is not skittish, he loves people, and he is the official greeter for classes at my home. It all worked out even in the city.

The point here is we may find ourselves at times doubting the information no matter how long we have been listening to it, acting on it and trusting it. My other point is, no matter how stubborn we get, if we truly want the answer it will keep repeating itself until we GET it! In addition, having Takota has been a joyful path, he has taught me many lessons, and this is a good sign of the higher good.

Is this all part of my soul path?

Absolutely. The lessons alone in getting Takota were priceless, and now that we have been together for three and a half years, I have found him to be my teacher ever since we met. All part of my soul path.

My soul purpose is that I am here to make a difference, and walking my soul path is my expression of myself while here on the earth. My path is my journey. Being on your soul path can mean different things to different people. For me it is growing, it is assisting others and the planet; it is walking my life in truth and wanting always to see the truth. It is seeing through illusions of life such as fear and lack. These are just a few. I do not believe anyone can tell you what it means, for it is an individual experience for all. My perception of what my soul path is has changed over the years as I have grown and changed and I believe it will continue to change.

There seems to be so many rules out there on what soul purpose is, all based on specific belief systems. I think belief systems are good and many may feel a need to belong to one. Even metaphysics or the New Age world has tons of different beliefs about the path. Whatever your belief, I know if you work on hearing your higher voice within and being aware of your connection with Source (no matter what your label for Source is); you will fully know what walking your path is in every given moment.

If you are wondering what will be your most joyful path of expression, as what will I do out there in the world, then start with what you love. List all the talents and qualities you have, if you are unsure ask a friend or two to list some things that stand out to them about you. If what comes into your mind feels like a natural thought or a small thought do not just let it pass, write them all down.

Making people laugh, a knack for noticing detail, a love for children, and a rapport with animals. Leave no stone unturned when knowing all the great things about you. After you have listed them all, list all the areas in life you can use these talents. List all of them without judging whether you think you can do them or not. Reach for the stars, stretch what your mind is telling you, and take it to the next level.

When I first started teaching what I know and what I have experienced in my walk in life, I had no thoughts of teaching it outside my home to people I did not know. People asked me that I did not know to teach and then by word of mouth, it spread and it became where I was asked to do talks all over and one of them was the University of Ohio, which I would have never imagined. So, do not judge, just reach for the stars and do not forget to add on the list, "or anything I have not thought of yet."

List all talents and qualities you know you have now. Do not leave anything out, it can be I color well or I love to bake. List them all.

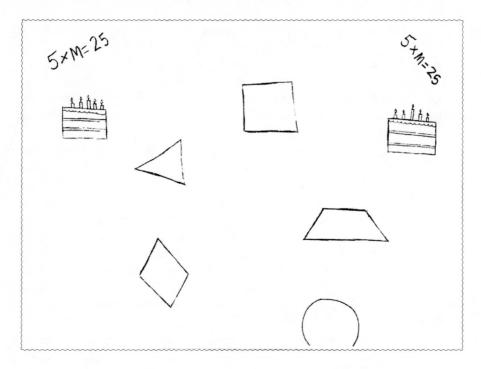

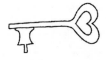

Keys to Sacred Space

- Honor You
- Honors Others and Their Path
- Make Meaningful Space for You

Sacred Space

As we are awakening and learning to work on our issues, heal down through the layers of our programs, and walk our true authentic selves, we need to remember to honor ourselves. As we change and grow, we develop healthy boundaries, we learn to say no and understand the difference of when we are truly helping someone, or we are disempowering them. We start to love our self more and in doing so we pamper and do nice things for us. When all these things occur, others around us who were used to the unhealthy you, will not like the changes at first. You are not over giving anymore, they were used to that, and you are a mirror of being healthy, which reflects to them what is not healthy in their life. That is scary for many people. We have to remember to be gentle with our selves and with others during our changes. Our changes also change the energies and environment that we live in, and how the ones around you choose to be in those changes, is their free choice. Many can act and want to grow and make changes within themselves, and others will react and emotionally deal with those changes in the way of resistance. Either way, you must honor yourself by not compromising your truths and not feeling responsible for how they choose to react. At the same time, it is important to also honor them and their choices with no judgment. You can allow and honor others' choices to want to react and still not choose to participate in their reaction.

When we begin to BE our true self, we perceive things differently around us and we make healthier choices for our selves. Many times during our transition we out grow friends and relatives, and sometimes mates. I do not mean outgrow in a way that says you never see them again, but you will be more discerning about what you engage in with them and what you choose not to. Many of my clients came from dysfunctional families and they had dynamics they played out with each other. We all have a role in our family unit. Many were the strong ones and the over givers and when they started choosing not to do things they knew were not healthy for either party, the family reacted, some would push every guilt button they could find to try and bring back out the old them, and others went as far as not to speak to them anymore. I know this can be very difficult for many, but look at the alternative. Would you want to consciously choose to go back into behavior that dishonored you, that was unhealthy, and that caused you to choose to compromise yourself? If you answered yes to that question, then my question to you would be why is it that you are consciously choosing self-abuse? That is what you would be doing. This is why on your journey of healing it is important to see yourself! Learn to know inside yourself that you are sacred space.

Yes, every part of your being is sacred space

Your body is the temple of your soul; your soul is an aspect of the life force energy of the ALL. Your mind is the power to create and manifest your reality. Mind, body, and spirit, you are sacred space. Of course, you would have to learn to love yourself before you could grasp this concept and begin to own it. But until you fully embrace this, you can create ways to bring the concept into your field until you can own it.

Let us start with your home, since it is a reflection of whom you are inside. It will most likely go through many changes as you grow and change inside. Look around the house now and ask yourself if it reflects who you are now. Then write down what you want to become. Write down where you see reflections in your house of how you are and who you are when fully awake. Imagine what being fully awake would feel like.

My house now and what it reflects:
I want my house to look like and to reflect:
Fully Awake I Feel:

Then decide to create just one room the way it is you see your future vision of you, the healthy and healed you. Everything in your life you put your essence into is sacred space. However, for now we want to work on a more conscious project like one room, so you can have a mirror of what you want to become to work with. It is a tool, and to have a focal point. Make this room feel like a nurturing and honoring room of what you want to achieve inside. Have fun with it, paint it the color that is soothing to you, and make it a non-stressful place where you feel safe and relaxed. Choose warm lighting; get big cushy pillows so you can hang out in this space comfortably. Maybe a small tabletop waterfall, lamps that you love, candles, aromas that make you feel warm and comfortable. Statues of people or pictures of places that bring you a good and healing feeling inside. Have fun decorating this space, a space just for you. Then spend some time in this room or space and just start feeling it and become the wonderful feeling that you have created here.

Many of you may not have a room you can do this with, but there is always a place you can find to do this for yourself if you want it badly enough. I lived in a four-bedroom house with my seven children. In my master bedroom, which was not terribly large, I took a shelf out and I built a sacred space in the corner of the room. You can put up a screen if you like with wonderful paintings on it; hang colorful scarves on the wall behind that space you are creating. Get creative; you can do it if you truly want it. Do it seasonally, in the spring and summer one of my sacred spaces was in the yard. I had created a corner with outdoor colored lights, ferns, and a waterfall. Go inside and find that part of you that yearns for the sacred space and let her/him out to create, create, and create. Get to know and feel this space for a while after you have created it. Go there to meditate, or write in your journal, dance, or just sit quietly with your waterfall sounds and aromas soothing your mind and spirit.

Now, after getting comfortable with your new space, I suggest putting a personal altar there, to honor you, your growth and to carry on it the things you are asking to work on inside.

I just heard and felt the gasps! An altar you say, and for myself, that is just wrong. I get this reaction from many people in the beginning until they start working with an altar and they feel and understand the space. Many feel this way depending on what beliefs you grew up with or in. In many beliefs an altar is only to someone we consider above us, more blessed and divine. Yet, if you really think about it, most of these people we put in this regard preached love, and preached we are all one and as powerful as they are. You have to decide for yourself how you feel about this. If you have too much of a problem with an altar for self, then just create a sacred space where you make a focus point of what you are working on inside. On the other hand, you may be at a place in your life, where you said Cool; I want that, sounds fun. Creating a personal altar can be fun and exciting, and you are the creator of the theme. First decide, do you want the altar to be a place where you are just honoring you as a Being? Do you want it to be a focal place where you make the energy of the altar represent what you are working on right now?

Have fun with the altar after you decide what you want to make the theme. Most times, my altar is what I want to work on inside myself. My very first altar was twenty-two years ago and I was working on healing my inner nine year old.

One thing I always did back then is after I knew what I was going to work on and make the altar about, I then asked my higher self to guide me to what I needed to put on my altar. Then I went spirit shopping, that is what I call it, because I feel it is going by spirit and not involving my ego or control. Allowing my intuition to guide me to where it wants to go. It is actually a lot of fun and adventuress, and spirit drives are great too. So, back to spirit shopping. I usually end up at a craft store, or an import shop but you never know. On my first altar, I found a miniature gilded birdcage, some small pines, and an ornament that was a little porcelain girl. For me the forest has always been my safe place and my nurturing place where I feel healed and nurtured. I made the altar look like a forest and to represent how I felt and where I wanted to go. I put the little cage up, set the girl in the doorway walking out to the forest, and had the door open. I had all the things I loved at nine years old around the forest. I always put an essential oil and a candle on my altar so that I use this space as a focus tool of what I am working on inside. I chose emotional healing oil at the time and a green tea candle for healing. I use my altar as a tool, a reflection of me now, where I want to go, and who I am. Every night before bed, I light a tea candle and incense, then meditate, and state my intentions of what I am working on or healing inside. I then go to bed, and upon waking, I always say a thankful prayer at my altar and take the old tea candle out. This routine assists me on beginning and ending my day of focused intent on my life and my day. As I felt the changes within me and as I worked on healing my inner nine year old, I would move the porcelain doll a few steps into the forest until she was lying in the forest happy and with the deer's. Once I have reached a place where I want to be with an issue, I change the altar theme.

After twenty-two years of doing this, my altars are very different now. I always have Quan Yin on the altar because for me she represents unconditional love and I am always striving for that in my heart. I add other things to it, change the décor as the seasons, and just get creative with it. What I have on my altar now is what I want to attract to me in my life.

The idea is to have fun with it and to look at it as a tool. It is no different from taping affirmations to your mirror; it is a focal point to keep putting your consciousness there. Why not for the inner self? All healing and change begins within. The inner work you are doing to better yourself, your life, and your journey can then be shared to improve the community, and then the world.

If you think you have no room in your house, I will say to you where there is a will there is a way. My children shared rooms and they had their own personal altars for a time. Since we were low on space with nine people in the house, I bought dinner plates to use as their altar space. Instead of a scarf, the kids would choose different colored tissue paper or wrapping paper, and tape it around the plate, and they would add miniature things on the plates for their themes. You can forfeit the candle until they are older.

Altars and special rooms are good things to start with to honor yourself and to understand that you are sacred space, and wherever you walk, you carry your sacred space with you. But as you walk this earth, and you do more inner work on your journey you begin to feel and know inside that all is sacred space and that each person's choices in life is their own unique sacred journey no matter what our thoughts are about their journey.

You begin to understand the oneness and the sacred journeys and you honor all of them.

When you first wake up and you are excited about what you have discovered about yourself and the universe, you want all your loved ones to get it too. You may become judgmental about their choices in life because now that you are exploring healthy choices you judge theirs as unhealthy and why wouldn't they want to change them? You can sometimes feel pushy at trying to assist one at seeing your newfound truths wanting them to see, feel, and know what you now know.

It is important as we walk our journey and we honor ourselves on that journey that we also honor all other being's journeys. There is no way we can know another's soul lessons here or the unique way in which they need to learn those lessons. Many times I do see people choosing what in my perception is the less joyful path and I wish for them that they awaken and choose more joyful ways to walk and learn their lessons, but I also know these are my perceptions from where I am and who I am now. Looking back, there was a day I also chose the less joyful road to my lessons, but I learned them. I am sure my many teachers in my life also thought of me, "I wish she would find the more joyful path." However, they were patient with me, they honored my journey, and this was the greatest gift of all from them.

> Just as we want others to honor our newfound changes in life, we also must honor their choices.

What is Sacred to You?
Draw or list it on this page.

SACRED SPACE

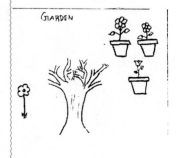

GARDEN

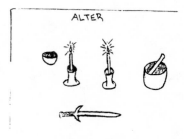

ALTER

Conclusion

Wishing You the Most Joyful Path

As we grow on the journey, we will start to see the honoring of all that is around us and how every step we take on this earth is sacred ground. Every beautiful sunset, waterfall, every encounter we have is sacred space. Everything in our world is an opportunity to learn and grow, and the greatest part is that we all have the freedom of choice in how we learn and what we share on the planet. Your journey to awaken your true heart is just beginning.

I wish you the most Joyful Path of your choosing and know, I SEE you and I honor every unique individual on this journey we share.

Love & Light!

A List of Resources

There are many modalities and services out there to further assist you in your healing and in your moving forward in life. I tell my clients, look around and pay attention to what you feel inside to be directed to the right tool for you. I am listing a few that I teach or that I have used and find work well for me. I also have listed some great reading material. I am in no way saying these will work for you also, just that I have used them, and again always go by what you feel.

ZENITH OMEGA has been poetically described as the "Language of Light". Zenith Omega utilizes the energy vibrations of each individual color and directs them into, through, and around the body, and the body's entire energy field.
Benefits of Zenith Omega Can be Expansive Some common effects are: An increased feeling & sense of well-being, Clarity of ideas & purpose, More self-confidence & personal power, Greater insight into one's self and others, Physical healings, Expansive abilities, Restoration of joy & laughter in life, Better communication & understanding in relationships, Feeling balanced & centered in a deepening experience of love
www.zenithexperience.net

Celestial Vibrations
Here you will find a synergy of wellness solutions to balance your life.
Please visit our website if you are looking for peace of mind, a healthy physical and emotional body, vibrational oil blends for your "Light" body, natural and safer products for your family, home, and the environment—even financial wellness!
http://www.celestialelements.com

Good Reading Material to Start:

The Dream Book by Betty Bethards

Heal Your Body by Louise L. Hay

All books by Doreen Virtue, Ph.D.

Channeling Biker Bob by Nik C. Coyler

Contact the author at

AnneAngelheart@aol.com or visit www.anneangelheart.com

978-0-595-49511-5
0-595-49511-7